Michael Chlistalla, Peter Gomber, and Torsten Schaper

THE FUTURE OF THE EUROPEAN POST-TRADING SYSTEM

A Delphi Study on the Future of the European Post-Trading System
in the Light of Globalization and the Financial Crisis

ibidem-Verlag
Stuttgart

Bibliografische Information der Deutschen Nationalbibliothek
Die Deutsche Nationalbibliothek verzeichnet diese Publikation in der Deutschen Nationalbibliografie; detaillierte bibliografische Daten sind im Internet über http://dnb.d-nb.de abrufbar.

Bibliographic information published by the Deutsche Nationalbibliothek
Die Deutsche Nationalbibliothek lists this publication in the Deutsche Nationalbibliografie; detailed bibliographic data are available in the Internet at http://dnb.d-nb.de.

∞

Gedruckt auf alterungsbeständigem, säurefreien Papier
Printed on acid-free paper

ISBN-10: 3-8382-0115-9

ISBN-13: 978-3-8382-0115-3

© *ibidem*-Verlag

Stuttgart 2010

Alle Rechte vorbehalten

Das Werk einschließlich aller seiner Teile ist urheberrechtlich geschützt. Jede Verwertung außerhalb der engen Grenzen des Urheberrechtsgesetzes ist ohne Zustimmung des Verlages unzulässig und strafbar. Dies gilt insbesondere für Vervielfältigungen, Übersetzungen, Mikroverfilmungen und elektronische Speicherformen sowie die Einspeicherung und Verarbeitung in elektronischen Systemen.

All rights reserved. No part of this publication may be reproduced, stored in or introduced into a retrieval system, or transmitted, in any form, or by any means (electronic, mechanical, photocopying, recording or otherwise) without the prior written permission of the publisher. Any person who does any unauthorized act in relation to this publication may be liable to criminal prosecution and civil claims for damages.

Printed in Germany

Acknowledgments

The authors are indebted to many people who have contributed to this study. Our thanks go to Dominik Adler (Association of German Banks), Marc Bayle (European Central Bank), Wilfried Blaschke (Commerzbank AG), Andrew Douglas (SWIFT scrl), Georg Fink (Oesterreichische Kontrollbank AG), Dorien Fransens (EuropeanIssuers), Kerstin Höltje (Eurex Clearing AG), Tomas Kindler (Link Up Markets), Mogens Kruse (VP Securities A/S), Vivian Mitropoulou (Hellenic Exchanges S.A.), Maik Neubauer (European Commodity Clearing AG), Ilse Peeters (Euroclear S.A.), Rafael Plata (Federation of European Securities Exchanges), Hilmar Schwarz (Deutsche WertpapierService Bank AG), Baris Serifsoy, Micha Sigloch (Consileon Business Consultancy GmbH), Meike Ströter (European Central Bank), Diego Valiante (Centre for European Policy Studies), Susanne Trimbath (STP Advisory Services LLC), and Geert Vanderbeeke (Fortis Bank Nederland NV), but to the same extent also to the many other participants who chose to remain anonymous.

E-Finance Lab

The E-Finance Lab is an industry-academic partnership between Frankfurt and Darmstadt Universities and partners BearingPoint, Deutsche Bank, Deutsche Börse, DZ Bank Gruppe, Finanz Informatik, IBM, T-Systems, 360 Treasury Systems, DAB bank and Interactive Data Managed Solutions located at Goethe-University, Frankfurt.

The goal of the E-Finance Lab is to jointly develop scientific yet managerial methods for rearranging the business processes of the financial service industry. The overall approach is to apply industrial methods well established in other domains, such as automotive supply chain optimization, to the financial supply chain.

Under the management of the professors of economics from Frankfurt University Peter Gomber, Andreas Hackethal, Wolfgang König, Bernd Skiera, and Mark Wahrenburg and informatics professor Ralf Steinmetz from Darmstadt University, 44 researchers work on improvements of the financial industry's value chain as well as of finance processes of companies from various industries. The development and testing of methods for designing innovative financial products is also part of the E-Finance Lab's research.

The concept of the E-Finance Lab illustrates that innovations in the financial industry are possible due to the usage of modern and net-based information and communication systems.

Management Summary

The European post-trading system has changed significantly in the last years and is currently facing enormous challenges, e.g. due to the financial crisis, stricter regulation of financial markets, globalization, and the automation of securities processing. Until now, a systematic assessment of the European post-trading industry is missing in academic literature. Using the Delphi methodology, this study among 158 experts from different areas of the post-trading industry aims to develop a joint and coherent view of how the European post-trading system will look like in the future. It identifies measures for improvement of the post-trading system and the most important issues in risk management and information technologies within this industry.

The assessment of *today's post-trading system* by the Delphi study expert panel turned out to be dichotomous: On the one hand, Europe's post-trading system is regarded efficient at the national level. On the other hand, the experts judge the European post-trading system to be rather inefficient at the cross-border level. In this context, the remaining Giovannini Barriers, but also deficiencies in the regulatory framework, were mentioned as the main reasons.

The *"ideal" European post-trading system* is characterized by the participants as one where all Giovannini barriers have completely been eliminated and where access and interoperability warrant the freedom of choice for investors in the area of trading, clearing, and settlement. Ideally, prices are kept low and innovation is kept high through sufficient competition, both on the trading and on the clearing level. The ideal regulatory framework, according to the panelists, focuses on functions rather than on institutions and distinguishes between the roles of market infrastructures and of financial entities taking credit risks. With reference to the financial crisis, participants claim that standardized OTC-products are ideally integrated into centralized clearing; in terms of the settlement infrastructure, their preferred solution is an integration of both the cash and the securities leg within a single settlement platform.

The participants of this study seem to be well aware that the ideal post-trading system as described above is still a long way off. Nevertheless, they do have a clear view of what the industry could realistically look like in 2020: The experts characterize the *future European post-trading system* as generally more integrated than today. Giovannini barriers are expected to be only partially removed: while the participants trust that technical, market practice and legal barriers will effectively be eliminated by 2020, the removal of the fiscal barriers is seen to require more time. With reference to the European Code of Conduct for Clearing and Settlement, the panelists anticipate price transparency and access and interoperability to be implemented in 2020. Despite of increasing integration of the industry, the experts do not think that there will only remain one single settlement institution; nor do they agree that there will be one user-owned and user-governed settlement infrastructure.

The experts propose a number of *measures for improvement* of the post-trading system that tackle both regulatory and organizational issues. They furthermore emphasize the importance of risk management and IT/IS for the sound functioning of the post-trading system. Although stating that financial infrastructures had been stable throughout the 2007-2009 financial crisis, the experts still see an urgent need for action in the area of risk management. IT/IS remains a key topic for the post-trading industry as the experts state that IT-systems continue to be an important competitive factor.

Table of Contents

Acknowledgments 5

Management Summary 7

1 Objective of the Study on the Future of the European Post-Trading System 11

2 The European Post-Trading System 17
    2.1 Processes and Institutions 17
    2.2 Network and Scale Effects in Clearing and Settlement 21
    2.3 Regulation and Market Initiatives in European Post-Trading 23
    2.4 The Financial Crisis 31

3 Delphi Study on the Future of the European Post-Trading System 32
    3.1 The Delphi Methodology 32
    3.2 Rationale for choosing the Delphi Methodology 33
    3.3 Setup of the Study 34
    3.4 Efficiency of the European Post-Trading System 43
    3.5 An Ideal European Post-Trading System 54
    3.6 The European Post-Trading System in the Future 63
    3.7 Measures to Improve the European Post-Trading System 75
    3.8 Risk Management Issues of the European Post-Trading System 83
    3.9 IT/IS Issues of the European Post-Trading System 90

4	Summary of Results and Outlook	96
5	References	103
6	Glossary	108
7	List of Tables	110
8	List of Figures	113
9	List of Abbreviations	115
10	Complete Results of Round Two and Round Three	117

1 Objective of the Study on the Future of the European Post-Trading System

The value of share trading on European securities markets has doubled in the last decade (WFE 2009). The share ownership structure in Europe is becoming more and more international as 37% of all stocks are held by foreign investors (FESE 2008). A growing proportion of trades is in foreign shares or by foreign investors, meaning that not only more transactions need to be settled, but more of these transactions require cross-border settlement. Moreover, the complexity of settlement rises with the increasing use of complex derivatives sometimes composed of multiple underlying assets from different trading venues. Trading activity, market liquidity, and capital market growth depend on safe and efficient trading and post-trading systems.

In the light of the 2007-2009 financial crisis, the importance of appropriate post-trading arrangements has gained even more weight and the focus of regulators and politicians is on ensuring the integrity, efficiency, and the greatest possible robustness of the post-trading system.

In context of our study, we define the term "post-trading system" as

> *the entirety of clearing and settlement institutions and additionally the providers of adjacent services such as custody and transaction banking.*

The related term of "post-trading activities", which has been specified by the European Commission (with the help of practitioners) in a 2005 working document, includes all those activities commonly referred to as "clearing and settlement". As these, however, have misleadingly narrow connotations, the European Commission's Definitions' Sub-Group recommends the term "post-trading activities", distinguishing between flow-related and stock-related activities (European Commission 2005). While flow-related activities refer to all activities that are transaction-dependent and which lead to the completion of the transaction, stock-related activities refer to activities which are linked to the security itself and are independent of the completion of the trade.

Institutions involved in the post-trading activities may include clearing houses and central counterparties (CCPs), central securities depositories (CSDs) and international central securities depositories (ICSDs) as well as intermediaries such as agent banks and global custodians, and further stakeholders such as the users (banks), exchanges, providers of technical infrastructures, the European and national central banks, and other supervisory authorities.

In contrast to a vast amount of academic research that traditionally focuses on the trading level with asset pricing and market microstructure theory as central topics, research with regard to the post-trading sector is rather sparse. Existing research on clearing, settlement, and custody issues or on the parties involved in these businesses regularly only addresses isolated factors, while a comprehensive view on the entire post-trading landscape is missing. The following table provides an overview of relevant academic literature in the area of securities post-trading activities.

Authors	Title / Research Subject and main Results
Schmiedel, Malkamäki, and Tarkka (2006)	*Economies of scale and technological development in securities depository and settlement systems* The authors investigate the existence of economies of scale in depository and settlement systems. The evidence from 16 settlement institutions for the years 1993-2000 indicates the existence of significant economies of scale depending on size of the institution and region. Small settlement service providers reveal a high potential of economies of scale, larger institutions show an increasing trend towards cost effectiveness. For clearing and settlement systems in countries in Europe and Asia substantially larger economies of scale are reported than those in the US system.

Serifsoy (2007)	*Stock exchange business models and their operative performance* Serifsoy analyzes technical efficiency and factor productivity of exchanges by investigating 28 stock exchanges from 1999-2003. His findings suggest that exchanges which diversify into related activities are mostly less efficient than exchanges that remain focused on the cash market. Moreover, his findings show no evidence that vertically integrated exchanges are more efficient than non-integrated exchanges.
Gomber and Schaper (2007)	*Impact of Information Technology on Settlement Services for Equities* The study investigates the status quo in the securities settlement industry especially concerning the usage of IT in this business area. The survey shows the diversity of the analyzed players in the settlement industry and highlights differences in their settlement processes and the usage of IT. The interviewed CSDs state to be mainly profit oriented and show increased growth rates in revenue and income for the analyzed time period from 2003 to 2005. Information technologies are playing an important role in the analyzed industry. Most CSDs are applying an integrated structure, providing services at different stages of the securities trading value chain, which consists of trading, clearing, and settlement.
Schaper and Chlistalla (2008)	*Competitive Clearing in Europe* The authors discuss competition among European clearing houses on their home markets. They apply the concept of the stakeholder value theory to this specific industry and derive a performance management system that includes financial and non-financial aims (e.g. risk) in context of competitive clearing.

Pirrong (2008)	*The Industrial Organization of Execution, Clearing and Settlement in Financial Markets*
	Pirrong analyzes the economics of securities trading, clearing, and settlement from a micro-analytic perspective. He discusses the existence of economies of scale in trading and post-trading applying theoretical analysis. Moreover, he demonstrates that especially in clearing strong scope economies exist. Furthermore, the impact of economies of scale and scope on the organization of these services is illustrated. As a central result, the paper reveals that the integration of trading and post-trading is the modal form of organization in financial markets.
Chlistalla and Schaper (2009); Schaper and Chlistalla (2009)	*Modifying the Balanced Scorecard for a Network Industry*
	- The Case of the Clearing Industry
	The authors modify the concept of the Balanced Scorecard to the specifics of a network industry. They develop a framework for the modification of the traditional Balanced Scorecard to fit the needs to the equities clearing sector. They emphasize the importance to include risk management and IT into the business strategy.
	- The Case of the Settlement Industry
	In a next research step they derive a Balanced Scorecard for the European Settlement Industry. The importance of IT and the need to monitor recent strategic projects are of particular importance and need to be included into the business strategy. They should therefore explicitly be incorporated within the Balanced Scorecard.
Pirrong (2009)	*The Economics of Clearing in Derivatives Markets*
	Pirrong conducts a comparative economic analysis of the costs and benefits of alternative default risk sharing mechanisms. His results cast considerable doubt on the advisability of central clearing of credit derivatives and demonstrate that clearing could actually increase risks to the broader financial system.

Oxera (2009)	*Monitoring Prices, Cost and Volumes of Trading and Post-trading Services*
	By providing a study on the prices, costs and volumes for trading and post-trading of securities in the EU, Oxera gives a detailed description of how the European capital markets are operating in terms of market dynamics as well as customer and supplier behavior. According to the paper, the costs of cross-border transactions in Europe are still between two and six times higher than domestic transactions. At the same time using infrastructure providers has become cheaper, by up to 80% over two years. This reflects significant price reductions as competition increases.

Table 1: Literature Overview

As outlined above, only singular items have been tackled by earlier researchers. Recent dynamics underline the need for a comprehensive view on the entire post-trading landscape. In an industry where a clear vision of how its preferred end state should look like is missing, it is fairly difficult for the involved parties to assess strategic directions for the future. The present work therefore intends to close this gap by developing a joint and coherent view of the future shape of the European post-trading system, taking into consideration the current challenges arising from the global financial crisis. We hope that our results may contribute to the current discussions and may be used to form the basis of such a vision.

To develop this vision, we aimed at having a panel of selected experts representing the various stakeholder groups outlined above discussing the following set of six questions. These are derived from literature, industry analyses and our previous work:

1. Do you think the current European post-trading system is efficient?

2. How do you expect the European post-trading system to look like ideally?
3. How do you expect the European post-trading system to look like in the future (e.g. in ten years)?
4. In the context of the global financial crisis: What are measures for improvement of the post-trading system?
5. What are the most important risk management issues the post-trading system needs to cope with?
6. What are the most important information technology / information system (IT/ IS) issues the post-trading system needs to cope with?

In the following, the results of a Delphi study among 158 post-trading experts are described. Chapter 2 introduces the European post-trading system and its characteristics. Chapter 3 as the main part of the document at hand gives a detailed description of the setup and the results of the Delphi study. The subsequent chapter concludes and gives an outlook.

2 The European Post-Trading System

Before presenting the approach and the results of our Delphi study, this chapter introduces the European post-trading system. Section 2.1 provides a short introduction into the most important processes and institutions in the post-trading industry. Section 2.2 discusses network and scale effects in clearing and settlement which have an impact on the efficient organization of the securities value chain. In the following section recent developments and regulation in European post-trading are discussed. Finally, the impact of the financial crisis on European post-trading is shown.

2.1 Processes and Institutions

Clearing and settlement are required after two parties have decided to transfer the ownership of a security. The purpose of clearing is the efficient handling of risks inherent to concluded, but still unfulfilled contracts. Clearing confirms the legal obligations from the trade. It involves the calculation of the mutual obligations of market participants and determines what each counterpart receives and what each counterpart has to deliver. Central counterparties can be included in the process of clearing. A CCP is an entity that interposes itself between the transactions of the counterparties in order to assume their rights and obligations, acting as a buyer to every seller and as a seller to every buyer. The original legal relationship between the buyer and the seller is thus replaced by two new legal relationships. The CCP absorbs the counterparty risk and guarantees clearing and settlement of the trade (Wendt 2006). Subsequent to the clearing stage, the second operation is settling a trade. Settlement is the exchange of cash or assets in return for other assets or cash and transference of ownership. A CSD is the organization that performs these functions (for more details see Giovannini Group 2001 and European Commission 2006).

The securities trading value chain consists of the complete set of relationships from investors to custody service providers, including the provision of all trading and post-trading activities. There are two types of activities in the trading and post-trading value chain: flow-related and stock-related activities. While flow-related activities are triggered by a trade on an execution venue, stock-related activities are independent from actual trades and relate to the holding of securities (e.g. corporate actions). Figure 1 shows that these are closely related, as the choice of market structures for the provision of stock-related activities will directly affect the market structures for flow-related activities (Oxera 2007).

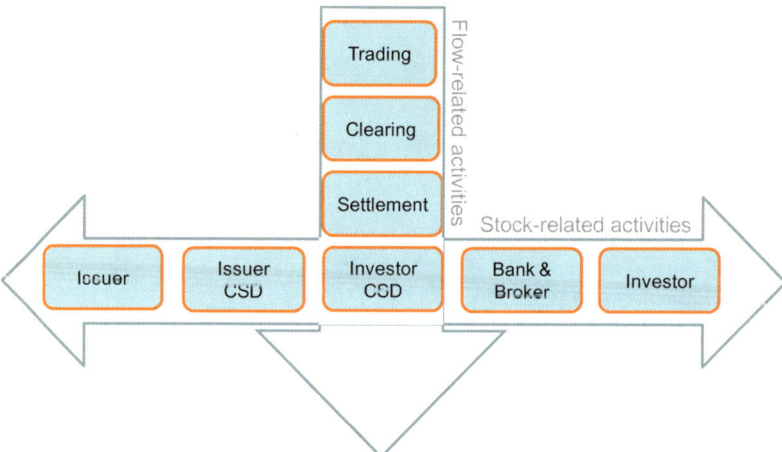

Figure 1: Flow-related and Stock-related Activities in the Securities Trading Value Chain (adapted from European Central Bank 2007)

Giovannini (2001) illustrates that cross-border clearing and settlement almost always involves several intermediaries in the transaction chain, implying a significantly greater degree of complexity in the process. The higher complexity of clearing and settling a cross-border transaction in comparison to a domestic transaction is explained in the following. In Figure 2 the instruction flow of a stylized domestic equity transaction is exemplified. It usually consists of six steps.

The Future of the European Post-Trading System 19

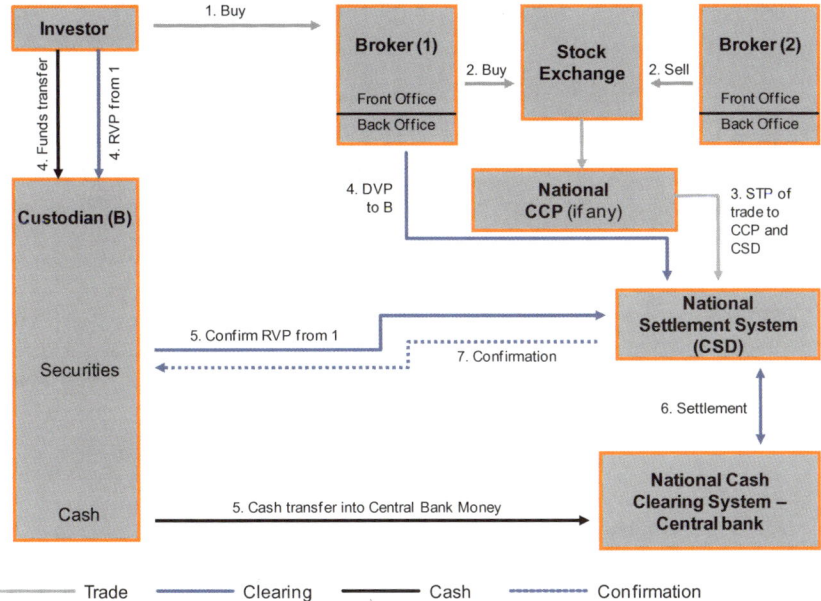

1. The transaction begins with the investor wishing to invest in a domestic equity. He contacts his broker (1) with an order to buy.
2. The broker (1) finds another broker (2) matching his order on the stock exchange.
3. The matched instruction transferring the equity from Broker (2) to Broker (1) may be sent to the CCP, if available, and is then sent on to the settlement system.
4. The investor forwards confirmation of the trade to his custodian (B), Broker (1) instructs delivery of equity to (B).
5. The custodian (B) confirms receipt of equity from Broker (1) and instructs delivery of cash.
6. The transaction is settled with the payment leg conducted via the central bank.

Figure 2: Instruction Flows for a domestic Equity Transaction (Giovannini Group 2001)

For a cross-border trade, investors rarely access a foreign system directly, but instead typically rely on intermediaries for this purpose. A cross-border transaction usually involves one of four basic models: using a link between two CSDs (the local and the foreign), using a network of local agents (who have access to the local CSDs), using a global custodian, or using an international CSD (ICSD). As a cross-border trade increases the number of clearing and settlement intermediaries that have to be accessed to complete the trade, this is likely to lead to high costs of a cross-border trade (NERA 2007) relative to a domestic trade. A stylized cross-border equities transaction instruction flow consists of nine steps (see Figure 3, for details see Giovannini Group 2001, pp. 9-15).

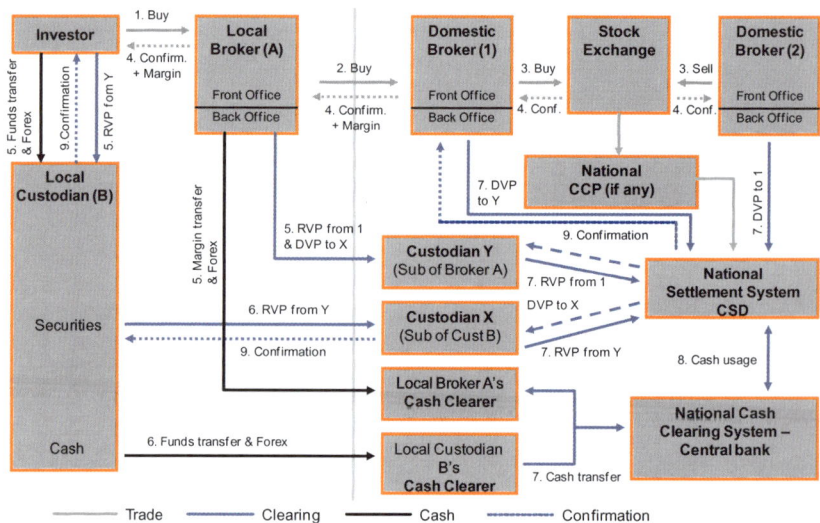

1. The transaction begins with the investor wishing to invest in a foreign equity. He will contact his local broker (A) with an order to buy.
2. Local broker (A) will forward the investor's order to his correspondent foreign-country broker (1).
3. The foreign-country broker (1) finds another foreign country broker (2) matching his order on the foreign-country stock exchange. The matched instruction may be sent to the CCP.
4. All agents receive and forward confirmation of the investor's order, while the instruction transferring the equity from (2) to (1) is usually sent automatically to the foreign-country CSD.
5. Local broker (A) instructs his foreign-country custodian (Y) to receive the equity from the foreign-country broker (1) and to deliver it to foreign-country custodian (X); the margin transfer (and foreign exchange conversion) from Broker A to the foreign-country CSD are conducted via the foreign-country cash clearer of local broker (A) and the foreign-country cash clearing system; the investor instructs his local

The Future of the European Post-Trading System 21

> custodian (B) to receive the equity from the foreign-country custodian (Y) of his local broker (A) and transfers the necessary funds for payment to his local custodian (B).
> 6. The local custodian (B) instructs its foreign-country custodian (X) to receive the equity from the foreign-country custodian (Y) of the local broker (A). The transfer of the investor's funds for payment is made from the local custodian (B) to its foreign-country cash clearer.
> 7. Foreign-country broker (1) receives the equity from foreign-country broker (2); then, foreign-country broker (1) delivers it to foreign-country custodian (Y), who delivers it to foreign-country custodian (X) – all within the settlement system of the foreign-country CSD; the foreign-country cash clearer of local broker (A) transfers funds for payment to the foreign-country CSD, while the foreign-country cash clearer of the local custodian (B) transfers the investors funds to the foreign-country cash-clearer of local broker (A).
> 8. The payment leg of the transaction is conducted via the foreign-country central bank.
> 9. Confirmation is then sent to all actors and equity transaction is booked (credit/debit) between foreign-country custodian (X) and local custodian (B) and between local custodian (B) and the investor.

Figure 3: Instruction Flows for a cross-Border Equity Transaction (Giovannini Group 2001)

2.2 Network and Scale Effects in Clearing and Settlement

Clearing and settlement are subject to network effects. Network effects arise in clearing because the greater the number of transaction counterparties that use the services of a CCP, the greater the probability that a transaction by a given party will be accepted by the CCP, and therefore the greater the utility for that party to buy the CCP services (European Commission 2006). Through multilateral netting the costs of collateral can be reduced. Network effects in settlement are existent in analogy to the telecommunication sector as settlement is a particular form of a telecommunications service (Knieps 2006): The greater the number of custodians connected to the CSD, the greater the network and therefore the utility for all users.

Economies of scale occur when firms achieve cost savings per unit by producing more units of a good or service. Such effects arise when it is possible to spread fixed costs over a higher output. The providers of trading, clearing, and settlement can achieve significant economies of scale, as the set-up costs for a transaction platform have a substantial portion of fixed costs and thus the average costs fall with an increasing transaction volume (Serifsoy and Weiß 2007). For the provision of a trading and post-trading infrastructure, high investments in IT infrastructure are necessary. These investments are largely independent from the number of transactions (Schaper 2009). Clearing houses have to create the necessary software and IT infrastructure. The costs of maintenance and operation of the clearing systems do not vary strongly with the number of transactions processed. Additionally, there are economies of scale in the main function of a clearing house - the bearing of risk. However, additional costs arise if there is more than one clearing house. In that case they need to manage the risk between the clearing houses and thus have to maintain costly communication links to the other clearing houses (Schaper 2009). Like trading and clearing, settlement requires the creation of software and IT infrastructure which involves a large fixed cost component (Schmiedel, Malkamäki, and Tarkka 2006).

Economies of scope occur when firms achieve cost savings by increasing the variety of goods and services they produce (joint production). Strong scope economies influence the efficient organization of trading, clearing, and settlement. These services require similar IT/IS infrastructures (e.g. datacenters, bandwidth, or connectivity) which provide potential for synergies. Scope economies may also originate from processing multiple products. For instance, if multiple asset classes are cleared within one clearing house the gains and losses can be netted across the customer's positions (Pirrong 2008). This cross-collateralization improves collateral efficiency and increases liquidity (European Commission 2009b).

2.3 Regulation and Market Initiatives in European Post-Trading

Compared with the US, the clearing and settlement industry in Europe is fragmented. Settlement in Europe has its origins in a patchwork of national systems. At the national level, consolidation has taken place and in most countries only one CSD has prevailed (Giovannini Group 2001). Domestic settlement systems are efficient within their national boundaries. The costs per transaction in domestic settlement are similar to the costs in the United States, but European CSDs realize higher margins (NERA 2004). In contrast, the settlement of cross-border transactions in Europe is not efficient because of various barriers (Giovannini 2001; Schmiedel, Malkamäki, and Tarkka 2006). The main reason for the fragmented European settlement industry is that historically securities were traded nationally, partly as a result of the existence of different currencies. In consequence, several CSDs at the European level continue to coexist and only recently consolidation has taken place. In the EU the number of settlement engines declined from 35 in 1999 to 27 in 2009[1]. During the same period of time, the number of clearing houses declined from 14 to 11[2]. Figure 4 shows the equity trading and post-trading market infrastructure in selected European countries. It illustrates that there is considerable vertical integration between providers of different trading and post-trading services.

---

[1] These figures include all EU accession rounds until 2009.

[2] This includes newly created CCPs.

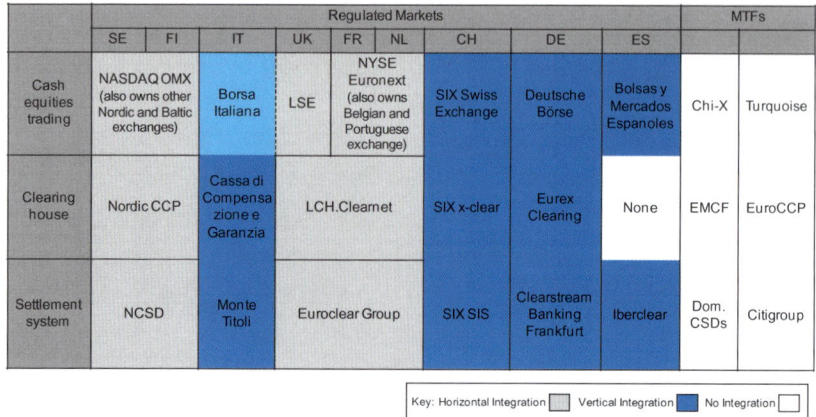

Figure 4: Selected Equity Market Infrastructures in Europe (adapted from Cox, Simpson, and Jones 2005)

The European post-trading industry is currently affected by regulatory initiatives (MiFID), market initiatives (Link Up Markets, SSE), and initiatives started by the European Commission or the Eurosystem (Code of Conduct, T2S) that are briefly portrayed in the following.

The **Markets in Financial Instruments Directive (MiFID)** is a European Union law which provides a homogeneous regulatory regime for investment services across the European Economic Area (European Commission 2004). The main objective of the directive is to increase competition and consumer protection in investment services. MiFID, which is part of the European Commission's 1999 Financial Services Action Plan (FSAP), replaces the Investment Services Directive of 1993 and has to be applied by investment firms and regulated markets since November 2007. By abolishing concentration rules, in which member states required investment firms to execute client orders on regulated markets only, MiFID allows new execution venues alongside established exchanges. In Article 34, MiFID regulates access to central counterparty, clearing and settlement facilities for investment firms and regulated markets. Chi-X, BATS, and Turquoise are examples of new trading platforms designed to rival incumbent exchanges. These new platforms bring competition into European securities trading and thus also into the clearing and settlement of cross-border transactions. As part of the 2010 MiFID review, the European Commission intends to reassess pre- and post-trade transparency requirements for non-equity markets, e.g. corporate bonds, structured finance products and credit derivatives and additional topics like the handling of so-called "dark pools" and the efficiency of the European best execution regime.

The **European Code of Conduct for Clearing and Settlement** (FESE, EACH, and ECSDA 2006) is a voluntary self-commitment of trading venues, CCPs, and CSDs in Europe and follows a number of principles on the provision of post-trading services for cash equities. The intention is to establish a strong European capital market and to allow investors the choice to trade any European security within a consistent, coherent, and efficient European framework. The Code of Conduct intends to offer market participants the freedom to choose their preferred provider of services separately at each layer of the securities trading value chain and to make the concept of cross-border redundant for transactions across EU member states. The implementation of the Code consisted of three phases, i.e. implementation of price transparency, access and interoperability, and service unbundling. It was implemented by the end of 2007. Especially access and interoperability, i.e. the second phase of the Code, is currently affecting the post-trade industry as the guidelines defined for access and interoperability provide the basis for the development of links between respective service providers. In total, more than 80 requests for access and interoperability can be counted. Progress has recently been considerable, with the Link Up Markets initiative on the settlement side (see below) and the arrival of EuroCCP and EMCF on the clearing side, which provide new clearing facilities and fuel competition among clearinghouses. In addition, LCH.Clearnet implemented interoperability with SIS x-clear after the LSE's decision to provide competing clearing services. Recently,

EuroCCP established interoperability with SIS x-clear for Turquoise's platform. In addition, several other competitive clearing deals have been agreed, like LCH.Clearnet for the European multilateral trading facilities (MTFs) BATS Europe, Chi-X, Turquoise, NYSE Arca Europe, and Nasdaq OMX (Lannoo and Valiante 2009).

TARGET2-Securities (T2S) is a proposal of the Eurosystem to European CSDs to transfer their securities accounts to a common technical platform. The main benefits of T2S would be the reduction of settlement engines and therefore the reduction of costs for CSD infrastructures and for custodians' back offices. The background of T2S is the technical debate about the best way to synchronize delivery of securities with the cash payment. The settlement of securities and cash would be realized within one single European platform. At the start of each day, participating CSDs would transfer their securities balances and outstanding transactions to T2S. During the day, T2S would settle these transactions and report to the CSDs at the end of the day. Figure 5 shows the current status with the TARGET2 payment system integrating the cash-side of the transaction and a number of DVP-links to the national settlement systems (top picture). In the bottom picture, the main difference by the introduction of T2S is shown: the integration of cash and securities settlement for all markets in one single technical platform.

In March 2007, the Governing Council of the European Central Bank concluded that it was feasible to implement T2S and therefore decided to proceed with the next phase of the project, namely the definition of user requirements on the basis of market contributions. These requirements were approved by the Governing Council. Most of the CSDs indicated participation and thus the Council decided in July 2008 to proceed with the project (European Central Bank 2008). In July 2009, 27 CSDs from 25 countries and the Eurosystem signed the T2S Memorandum of Understanding. These include the CSDs in all euro area countries as well as nine non-euro area CSDs. The final version of the general functional specifications was published in November 2009 (European Central Bank 2009). Details of T2S, like supervision of the platform, governance, questions on competition, the effects on the private enterprise infrastructure, and alternatives to integrate the different national infrastructures (LIBA, ESF, and ICMA 2007) remain to be clarified in the near future.

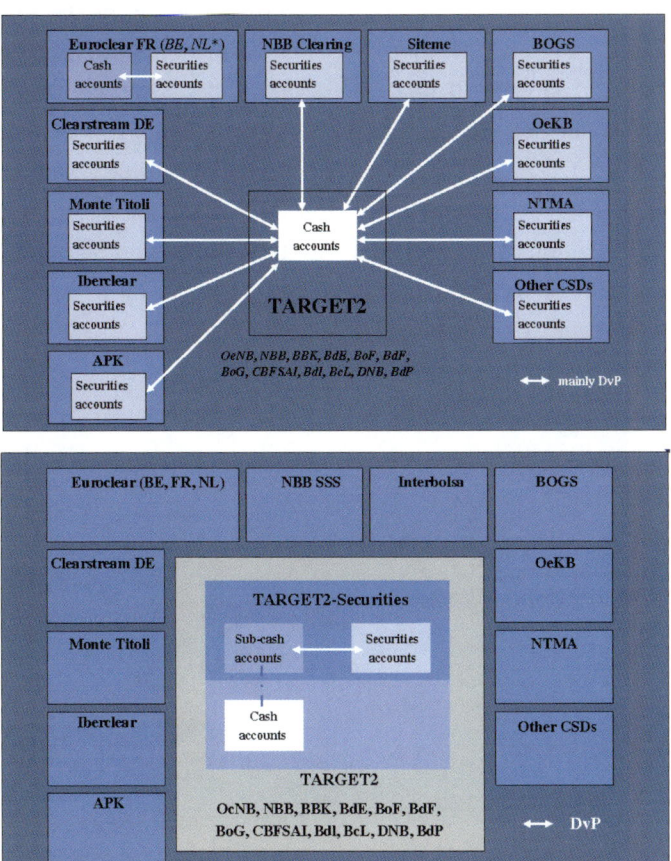

Figure 5: Integration of Payment and Settlement System with TARGET2 and TARGET2-Securities (European Central Bank 2006, Tumpel-Gugerell 2006)

Link Up Markets is a joint venture by eight European CSDs and one non-European CSD aiming to create a technical platform which links together multiple CSD markets. The idea is to overcome hurdles and inefficiencies in cross-border equities business by establishing a single cross-border operating organization. Link Up Markets plans to deliver a central linkage to the national systems. While CSDs will still provide the single point of access for customers in case of domestic and cross-border business (Link Up Markets 2009) and all domestic institutions and infrastructures will remain unchanged, savings are expected as only one organization is to implement and to manage the cross-border network. Settlement will take place in the issuer CSD, warranting that regulatory requirements are met. Since CSDs are exclusive clients of the Link Up Markets platform, only the CSD of choice is responsible for handling the relationship with its customers. Market participants will settle across borders via their domestic entry into this structure. The need to maintain several different access points will thus recede (see Figure 6).

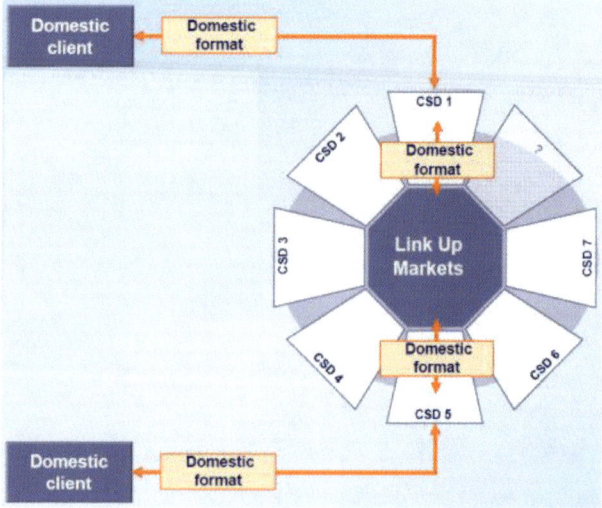

Figure 6: Link Up Markets Interaction Channels (Link Up Markets 2009)

Each domestic CSD retains its current state and function and all access points can still be used. Reduced interconnection costs are expected regarding negotiations, link processing, interfaces, synchronization of systems, data formats, link contracts, liquidity requirements, and effective use of collateral. In addition, Link Up Markets will achieve network externalities leading to further cost savings shared by the whole community, as centralized linkage will help in standardizing processes and practices (Link Up Markets 2009). The platform provides a basis for further consolidation and integration of the European capital market, because the linkage of domestic systems increases the pressure to apply common technical standards, harmonized rules and regulations, identical tax treatment, and handling of country-specific taxes. The first markets have gone live in March 2009 with six CSDs connected as of December 2009.

The **Single Settlement Engine (SSE)** is an integration project of the Euroclear Group. Instead of achieving interoperability of the different national systems, Euroclear is implementing an integrated platform for securities settlement in Belgium, France, the Netherlands, Ireland, and the UK. The SSE is a practical harmonization project that already today provides integrated cash and securities settlement. It merges five settlement platforms into one, thereby accomplishing Euroclear's objective of harmonizing services on a consolidated processing platform. Users of the SSE operate as if they would act in a domestic market.

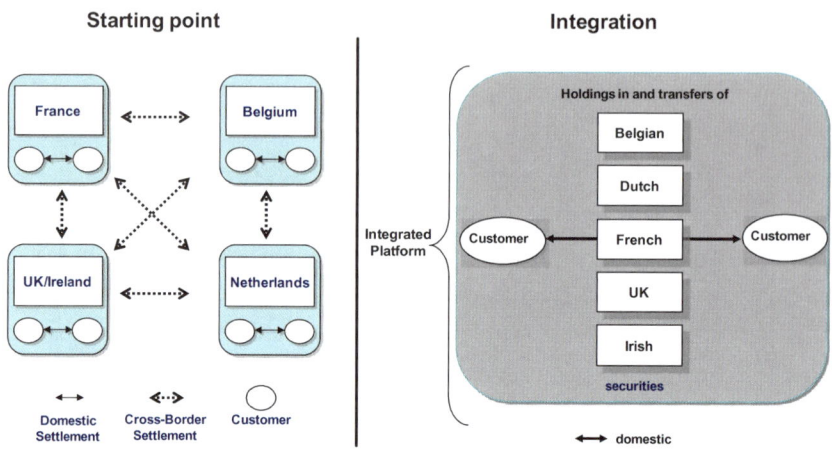

Figure 7: The Single Settlement Engine (Euroclear 2002)

The next step in Euroclear's migration to a single platform is the launch of **Euroclear Settlement for Euronext-zone Securities (ESES)**. Using the SSE as its foundation, ESES will serve as a single processing solution to process both domestic and cross-border fixed-income and equity transactions in the Belgian, Dutch, and French markets as If they were a single market. ESES was launched in France at the end of 2007, and in Belgium and the Netherlands in the second quarter of 2008. The final consolidation of the platforms is aimed for 2010. Euroclear has announced to acquire the Nordic CSD and to extend the SSE to these markets (Finland and Sweden) as well.

2.4 The Financial Crisis

The 2007-2009 financial crisis has brought OTC derivatives at the forefront of regulatory attention. OTC derivatives, especially Credit Default Swaps (CDS), played a significant role as originators of the crisis. The financial market turbulence illustrated that the absence of adequate post-trading infrastructure contributes to weaknesses in operational and counterparty risk management. A lack of transparency and oversight in OTC derivatives markets with negative implications for overall financial market functioning and financial stability was observed. OTC derivatives markets seem to have acted as a contagion channel during the crisis, because of a lack of information about where risks related to OTC derivatives arose and how they were distributed through the financial system. OTC derivatives markets are large in size and closely linked to the cash markets (European Central Bank 2009b). In order to improve financial stability in derivatives markets, the European Commission has called for concrete proposals how to mitigate the risks associated with credit derivatives. Key priority was given to the effective implementation and usage of CCPs for CDS within the euro area. As a result, CDS dealers committed to start clearing eligible CDS through European CCPs starting 31st July 2009 (European Commission 2009). The development of post-trading infrastructures for OTC derivative markets should be accompanied by enhanced cross-border cooperation among authorities in order to achieve a consistent regulatory framework for different infrastructures (European Central Bank 2009b).[3]

---

[3] As the process of designing the future regulatory framework is currently changing nearly on a daily basis, we encourage the reader to refer to the website of the European Commission for further information.

3 Delphi Study on the Future of the European Post-Trading System

This chapter gives a detailed description of the setup and the results of the Delphi study. First, a brief introduction into the Delphi study methodology and the rationale for choosing this methodology are presented. Then the setup of the study - design, participants, and response rates – is described. In the following sections, the results of the six research questions discussed with the experts are detailed.

3.1 The Delphi Methodology

The Delphi methodology is a group facilitation technique in the form of an iterative multi-stage process designed to transform individual opinions into group consensus. It is a flexible approach commonly used within the social sciences (Hasson, Keeney, and McKeena 2000). This technique seeks to obtain the opinions of experts through a series of structured questionnaires (referred to as "rounds") or interviews. The initial questionnaire may also collect qualitative comments. After each of these rounds and following statistical analysis regarding group collective opinion, the results are fed back in a structured questionnaire to the previous round's participants who are then asked to reassess these results. This process is ongoing until consensus is obtained or diminishing returns can be observed (Hasson, Keeney, and McKeena 2000).

In his seminal work on methods for decision making, Dalkey (1969) describes the results of an extensive set of experiments conducted in order to evaluate the effectiveness of the Delphi procedures for formulating group judgments. Dalkey focuses on the three features of the Delphi procedures:

1. Anonymous response: opinions of members of the group are obtained by a formal questionnaire;

2. Iteration and controlled feedback: interaction is effected by a systematic exercise conducted in several iterations, with carefully controlled feedback between rounds; and

3. Statistical group response: the group opinion is defined as an appropriate aggregate of individual opinions in the final round.

One of the most significant benefits of the Delphi methodology is the fact that the researcher does not need to bring the interviewees together physically. This guarantees that the participants cannot influence each other directly. Nevertheless, they retain the opportunity to change their opinions in later rounds when realizing from the collective opinion that they may have missed items or thought them unimportant (Couper 1984).

Controversial debate rages over the use of the term "expert" and how to identify a professional as an expert. Hasson, Keeney, and McKeena (2000) therefore point out the importance of a fine balance among the expert panel.

3.2 Rationale for choosing the Delphi Methodology

In our previous research (Gomber and Schaper 2007; Chlistalla and Schaper 2008, 2009) we have found that Europe's post-trading environment is becoming more competitive since domestic and cross-border trading on securities markets have increased significantly over the last decade. This means that not only more transactions need to be settled, but more of these transactions require cross-border settlement. In the course of the financial crisis some of the financial infrastructures had to handle enormous peaks in volumes: for instance, the settlement system of the UK (Euroclear) had to handle 1.6 million transactions on a single day, double the average monthly volume (Francotte 2009). Clearing and settlement systems must be designed to minimize operational risks as well as the systemic risk (e.g. in case of the Lehman default) of securities transactions. Risk management and IT are important drivers for managing these challenges efficiently, but have not been discussed systematically yet.

Since the nature of our research questions required a broad set of opinions from true subject-matter experts to be collected, we decided in favor of the Delphi methodology. Moreover, there are a limited number of experts in this field and it is extremely difficult to find interview partners or study participants who are willing to share their knowledge and expertise due to the competitive and regulatory sensitivity of these issues.

3.3 Setup of the Study

Participants' Identification and consecutive Rounds of the Study

In order to define the scale and scope of the Delphi study, as a first step an industry analysis was performed. Stakeholders that are involved within the securities trading value chain were considered, i.e. in trading, clearing, settlement or in adjacent services such as custody and transaction banking. A stakeholder is any group or individual who can affect or is affected by the achievement of the organization's objectives. To affect the firm means to have the power to influence the company. To be affected by the firm results in the fact that these groups or individuals have an interest in or claim on the company, because they are involved in the operation of the firm. Thus, two attributes can be defined to identify stakeholders: power to influence the firm and the legitimate claim or interest in the firm (Freeman 1984). Dominant stakeholders are both powerful and have a legitimate claim or interest in the firm. These stakeholders are the key stakeholders that actually draw the attention of the management. They are important for managers, because their claims or interest in the firm are justified by the legitimacy of their relationship with the firm. In addition, they have the capacity to force the firm to take account of their claims (Mitchell, Agle, and Wood 1997).

In context of this study a stakeholder analysis was performed to identify relevant stakeholders of institutions in the post-trading system. Figure 8 shows the stakeholders across these institutions.

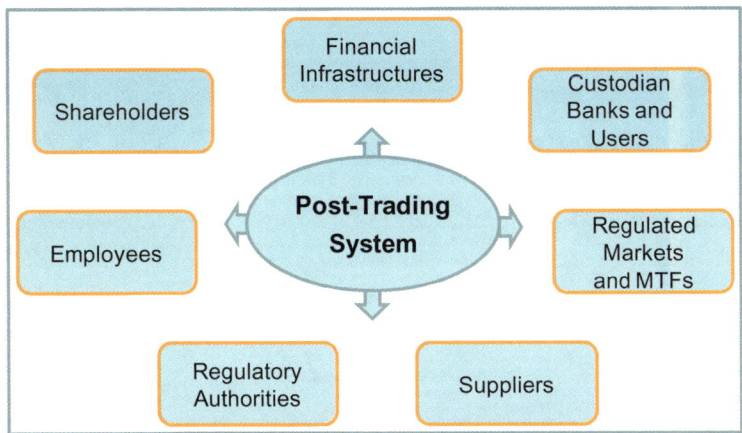

Figure 8: Stakeholders of the European Post-Trading System

Seven categories of expert groups were identified for the Delphi study on the European post-trading system: five of the above stakeholder groups plus experts from academics and associations. These are (1) financial infrastructures (clearing houses, CSDs, and ICSDs), (2) regulated markets and MTFs, (3) custodian banks and users of financial infrastructures, (4) regulatory authorities (e.g. central banks), (5) suppliers (e.g. consultancies and technical infrastructures), (6) academics and researchers, and (7) associations (including issuers and investor associations).

For the composition of the study's participant panel, we identified between 15 and 25 industry experts per above-mentioned category. The interviewees were selected from participant lists of relevant institutionalized groups such as the Code of Conduct Monitoring Group (MOG), the T2S Advisory Group and its various sub-groups, or the European Commission's Clearing and Settlement Advisory and Monitoring Expert groups (CESAME and CESAME2) as found on the relevant websites.

In case of multiple potential interviewees, participants were selected according to their hierarchy within their institution and according to their assumed expertise in terms of securities trading and/or post-trading. Moreover, we identified a number of experts by reviewing academic as well as practitioners' publications and presentations on post-trading. Potential participants finally summed up to 158.

The Delphi study was designed as an online survey (see Figure 9) allowing contributors to self-register and to participate at any point in time between April and September 2009. The survey was implemented with Java Server Pages and Java Beans using open-source software for the deployment and the operation of the study.

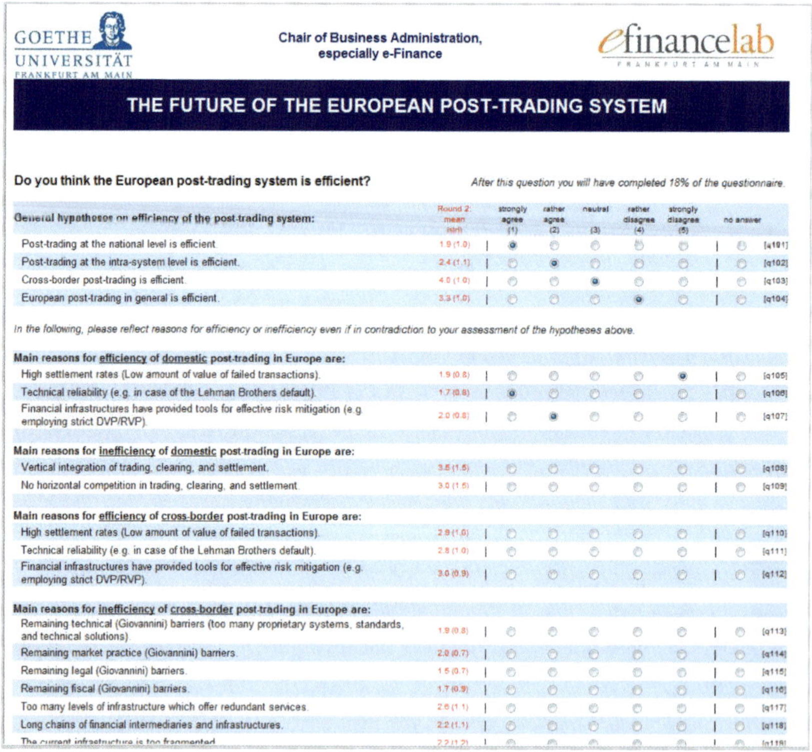

Figure 9: Screenshot of the Online-Survey

The study consisted of three consecutive rounds. The objective of round one was to generate the hypotheses for assessment in the subsequent rounds. As in a classical Delphi study, round one began with an open-ended set of questions that generated ideas and allowed participants complete freedom in their responses. This helped to identify issues which would be addressed in subsequent rounds (Gibson 1998). Participants were encouraged to contribute with as many opinions as possible so as to maximize the chance of covering the most important opinions and issues (Hasson, Keeney, and McKeena 2000). The experts were asked open questions on six topics on and around post-trading (see Table 2).

Round two was made up of the analysis of the results of round one. Therefore, the answers from the first round were analyzed and transformed into hypotheses, which were then presented to the experts in round two. Data analysis involves the analysis and careful management of qualitative and quantitative data (Hasson, Keeney, and McKeena 2000). In our case, quite extensive amounts of qualitative data were generated: The outcome of the first round amounted to 595 hypotheses and 21,000 words. During the analysis process, duplicate answers were eliminated and similar items were grouped together according to a coding scheme developed during the process. In order not to influence the participants, this coding scheme was not communicated to the panel in round two. As Hasson, Keeney, and McKeena (2000) propose, no items should be added during analysis and the wording used by participants, with minor editing, should be used as much as possible for round two. No items were added and only very few statements were dropped where either the meaning was entirely unclear or where apparently sentences had been left incomplete by the study participant. Where different terms were used for what appeared to be the same issue, they were grouped together in an attempt to provide unambiguous descriptions. Finally, 191 hypotheses were derived in total, which distribute across the individual questions from round one as shown in Table 2.

Additionally, the participants were given the possibility to comment their answers within text fields provided for remarks or comments.

Initial open Questions in Round 1		Number of Hypotheses in R2 and R3
Question 1	Do you think the current European post-trading system is efficient? Please explain.	35
Question 2	How would the European post-trading system look like ideally?	30
Question 3	How do you expect the European post-trading system to look like in the future (e.g. in ten years)?	47 (48 in round 3)
Question 4	In the context of the global financial crisis: What are measures for improvement of the post-trading system?	35
Question 5	What are the most important risk management issues the post-trading system needs to cope with?	23
Question 6	What are the most important IT/ IS issues the post-trading system needs to cope with?	20

Table 2: Questions and Hypotheses of the Delphi Study

In round three the participants were provided the results of the analysis of round two's responses with corresponding statistical information (mean and standard deviation) presented to indicate first trends towards collective opinion.

Before starting each round, a series of pre-tests with selected participants of the study was conducted in order to assure intuitiveness of the online tool and comprehensibility of the questions and hypotheses. Per round, the feedback from three pre-tests was incorporated. For instance, minor edits on a small number of statements in order to clarify certain hypotheses were performed; especially with regard to the first question, related hypotheses were clustered into groups; the navigation through the online questionnaire was improved by adding the possibility to move forward and backward; initial guidance was given about the number and direction of questions to be answered. A more detailed definition of the term "post-trading system" was presented and the scope of the study was elaborated.

We guaranteed the participants that any statements or comments provided during the entire course of the study would be treated and used confidentially and in an anonymous way. They were also asked whether we were allowed to report individuals' participation in the study, which was agreed by 20 panelists (see Acknowledgments).

Registration for participation in the study was open beginning April 28th 2009. The experts were initially given a period of three weeks per round to answer the questions, which was extended by another two weeks per round to account for holiday season and other absences. The Delphi survey was finally closed on September 25th 2009.

Overview of participants and response rates

The following Table 3 shows the number of participants per round and per expert group. Upon their registration, the participants were requested to provide details on their affiliation, position, and the number of years of industry expertise. They were also asked to select from a list of categories the perspective from which they would be answering the questionnaire. The mean industry expertise of the panel is 12.5 years. On average, 94 percent of the hypotheses were rated by the participants.

Of the 158 experts contacted in round one, 42 from 15 countries took part. In rounds two and three all participants of the first round plus another three individuals identified as industry experts in the meantime were included. Some participants deliberately missed out on round two and re-joined the study for the final round. This explains e.g. the drop in

Table 3 from 14 to 9 in the "Financial Infrastructures" group between round one and round two and the rise from 9 to 12 participants between round two and round three. The response rates of the last two rounds were over 80 percent of the sample.

	Round 1 (N=158)	Round 2 (N=45)	Round 3 (N=45)
Financial Infrastructures	14	9	12
Custodian Banks / Users	7	5	6
Supervisory Authorities	5	6	6
Academics	4	5	6
Consultancies / Technical Infrastructures	4	4	3
Associations	4	4	4
Regulated Markets / MTFs	4	3	3
Total	42	36	40
Response rate	27%	80%	89%

Table 3: Participants and Response Rates

Interestingly, the means of the single hypotheses did not diverge very much between round two and round three. It is worth mentioning that more than 15 percent of the answers were modified by the participants and the standard deviation in total has decreased, which indicates consensus building. Only 20 percent of the participants did not change any answers in round three.

For the assessment of the hypotheses a 5-item Likert scale was provided with the following attributes: "strongly agree", "rather agree", "neutral", "rather disagree" and "strongly disagree" plus an additional option "no answer" to be ticked in case the individual intentionally did not want to provide an opinion regarding a certain statement (see Figure 10).

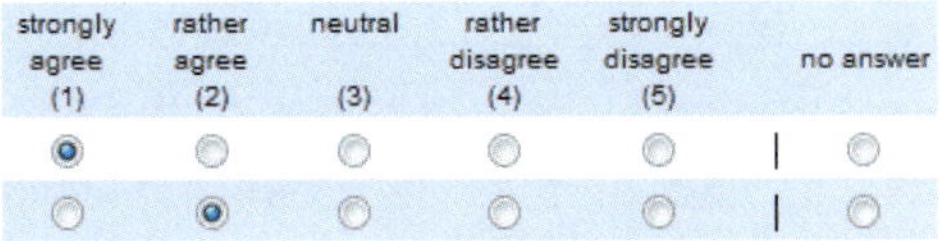

Figure 10: 5-Item Likert Scale

For the purpose of providing mean and standard deviation (STD) within this report, each attribute was assigned a value ranging from 1 for "strongly agree" to 5 for "strongly disagree". "No answer" was assigned the value zero and was not considered for the statistical analysis.

Structure of the Result Presentation

In the subsequent sections an analysis of the study's results will be presented. The focus is on the final assessments, i.e. on the results from round three. Only in case of significant changes of the group opinion between round two and three these will be mentioned and analyzed. An exhaustive overview of all results (from rounds two and three) is provided in the appendix. Consideration must be given to the level of consensus to be employed. A universally agreed proportion does not exist for the Delphi methodology (Hasson, Keeney, and McKeena 2000). Details will therefore be provided according to the following criteria:

- The focus of the analysis lies on the mean. Those hypotheses with agreement (mean ≤ 2.0) and disagreement (mean ≥ 4.0) will be described in detail and incorporated in the formation of the coherent views. All items with a mean ≤ 2.0 or ≥ 4.0 will be highlighted in light grey color in the result tables.
- Hypotheses with a high STD (≥ 1.2) will be highlighted in dark grey color in the result tables and will be analyzed in detail concerning the assessment of different experts groups (e.g. financial infrastructures, supervisory authorities etc.) as a broad variation in the answers can often be traced back to different groups of individuals having different opinions.

- In addition, hypotheses will be analyzed that are fundamental for the post-trading system (e.g. due to the frequency of similar answers in the first round or the status in public discussions).

The subchapters are closed with an intermediate summary on the main consistent views (i.e. those with a mean ≤ 2.0 or ≥ 4.0) among the participants of the study as well as additional quotes that were provided by single experts.

For the remainder of this report, the terms *experts*, *participants* and *panelists* will be used synonymously.

3.4 Efficiency of the European Post-Trading System

The objective of the survey's opening question of round one was to receive an impression of the panelists' attitude towards the efficiency of the European post-trading system. We therefore started with a set of hypotheses regarding the efficiency of the European post-trading system at different levels. This first block of hypotheses (see Table 4) was answered by nearly all participants. The experts rather agree that Europe's post-trading system at the national level is efficient [mean = 1.95]. To a lower extent they also agree that the post-trading system is efficient at the intra-system level (in contrast to the purely national level) [2.45]. When it comes to the cross-border level, the participants rather disagree regarding its efficiency [4.05]. Concerning the efficiency of the European post-trading system in general the experts are neutral with a tendency towards rather disagreeing [3.25].

	General hypotheses on efficiency of the post-trading system:	Mean	STD	n (N=40)
1-01[4]	Post-trading at the national level is efficient.	1.95	0.96	40
1-02	Post-trading at the intra-system level is efficient.	2.45	1.13	38
1-03	Cross-border post-trading is efficient.	4.05	1.00	39
1-04	European post-trading in general is efficient.	3.25	0.93	40

Table 4: General Hypotheses on the Efficiency of the Post-Trading System

---

[4] The respective first columns of the following tables contain the numbering of the hypotheses as used in the questionnaire.

For the remaining hypotheses we asked the participants to reflect reasons for efficiency or inefficiency even if in contradiction to their assessment of the hypotheses above.

The second block of hypotheses addresses main reasons for the <u>efficiency</u> of <u>domestic</u> post-trading in Europe (see Table 5). The experts rather agree that high domestic settlement rates within Europe's post-trading system, its technical reliability and the fact that financial infrastructures have provided tools for effective risk mitigation are main reasons for the systems domestic efficiency. In total, there is a strong consent in these opinions (which is indicated by a low STD ranging from 0.62 to 0.87 only).

	Main reasons for efficiency of domestic post-trading in Europe are:	Mean	STD	n (N=40)
1-06	Technical reliability (e.g. in case of the Lehman Brothers default).	1.79	0.78	38
1-07	Financial infrastructures have provided tools for effective risk mitigation (e.g. employing strict DVP/RVP).	1.87	0.62	38
1-05	High settlement rates (Low amount of value of failed transactions).	1.95	0.87	38

Table 5: Reasons for the Efficiency of the domestic Post-Trading System in Europe

The third group of hypotheses addresses reasons for the inefficiency of domestic post-trading in Europe (see Table 6). The survey participants are neutral [3.03] with regard to the thesis that no horizontal competition in trading, clearing, and settlement is a main reason for the inefficiency of the domestic post-trading system. The high STD again indicates little consensus among the experts. Looking at their answers in more detail we notice that the majority of experts from financial infrastructures and regulated markets rather or strongly disagree [3.73], while all other experts are neutral or rather agree [2.60]. This observation is depicted in Figure 11 (the axis of ordinate shows the absolute number of answers).

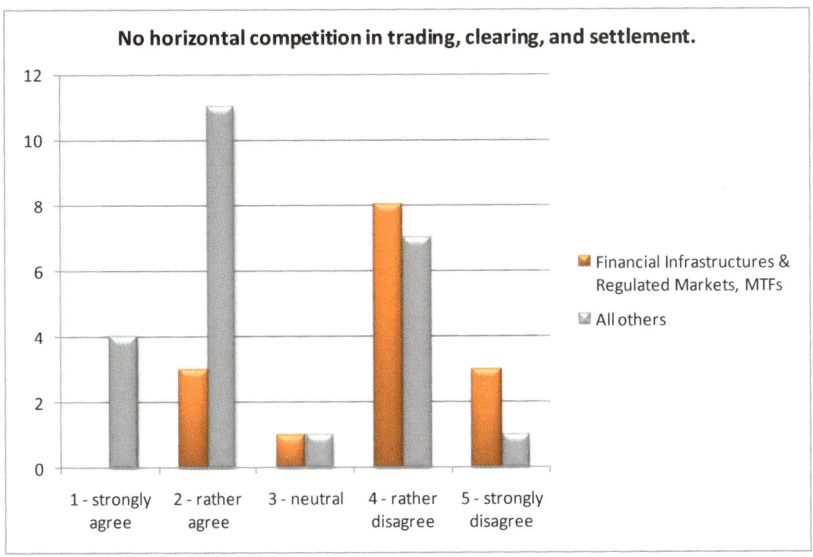

Figure 11: Distribution of Answers regarding Hypothesis 1-09

Moreover, the experts rather disagree [3.50] that vertical integration of trading, clearing, and settlement is a main reason for inefficiency. The high STD in this case shows that there is not much consensus among the experts. Looking at the answers in more detail we observe that the experts from financial infrastructures and regulated markets rather disagree [4.20], while the rest of the panel is neutral [3.09] (see Figure 12).

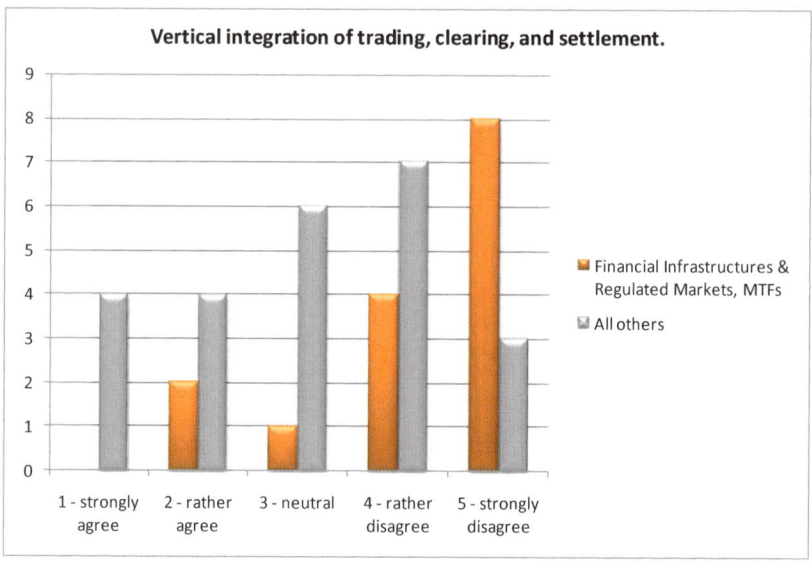

Figure 12: Distribution of Answers regarding Hypothesis 1-08

	Main reasons for inefficiency of domestic post-trading in Europe are:	Mean	STD	n (N=40)
1-09	No horizontal competition in trading, clearing, and settlement.	3.03	1.27	39
1-08	Vertical integration of trading, clearing, and settlement.	3.50	1.34	39

Table 6: Reasons for the Inefficiency of the domestic Post-Trading System in Europe

The next group of hypotheses addresses main reasons for the efficiency of cross-border post-trading in Europe. The experts are neutral with regard to the following three hypotheses (see Table 7). One main reason for this might be that the experts rather disagreed to the earlier hypothesis of the cross-border post-trading system being efficient (see hypothesis 1-03 in the first block above), which might also explain why

17 percent (13 percent) of the participants did not answer this question in the second (third) round.

	Main reasons for efficiency of cross-border post-trading in Europe are:	Mean	STD	n (N=40)
1-11	Technical reliability (e.g. in case of the Lehman Brothers default).	2.80	0.87	35
1-12	Financial infrastructures have provided tools for effective risk mitigation (e.g. employing strict DVP/RVP).	2.97	0.89	35
1-10	High settlement rates (Low amount of value of failed transactions).	3.03	0.92	35

Table 7: Reasons for the Efficiency of the cross-border Post-Trading System in Europe

Next, the main reasons for the inefficiency of cross-border post-trading in Europe were investigated (see Table 8). There is a common understanding among our expert panel that the remaining Giovannini Barriers are main reasons for the inefficiency of cross-border transactions. They may be ranked in the following order: almost strong agreement with regard to legal barriers [1.51] and rather agreement with regard to fiscal barriers [1.71], technical barriers [1.85], and market practice barriers [1.90].

	Main reasons for inefficiency of cross-border post-trading in Europe are:	Mean	STD	n (N=40)
1-15	Remaining legal (Giovannini) barriers.	1.51	0.76	39
1-16	Remaining fiscal (Giovannini) barriers.	1.71	0.84	39
1-13	Remaining technical (Giovannini) barriers (too many proprietary systems, standards, and technical solutions).	1.85	0.74	39
1-14	Remaining market practice (Giovannini) barriers.	1.90	0.68	39

Table 8: Reasons for the Inefficiency of the cross-border Post-Trading System in Europe: Giovannini Barriers

Concerning the remaining hypotheses on the inefficiency of cross-border post-trading, only the most interesting ones are highlighted here. A complete and detailed overview is presented in the following tables. None of the hypotheses was disagreed to.

The experts rather agree with tendencies towards strong agreement [1.70] that some financial intermediaries and infrastructures generate revenues from the inefficiencies (see Table 9). In this context, they rather agree that "long chains of financial intermediaries and infrastructures" [2.08], the fact that the "current financial infrastructure is too fragmented", and that there is a "lack of interoperability between financial infrastructures" [both 2.13] as well as "limited competition" [2.28] are further reasons for the inefficiency of cross-border post-trading.

	Main reasons for inefficiency of cross-border post-trading in Europe are:	Mean	STD	n (N=40)
1-22	Some financial intermediaries and infrastructures generate revenues from the inefficiencies.	1.70	0.85	37
1-18	Long chains of financial intermediaries and infrastructures.	2.08	0.96	39
1-19	The current infrastructure is too fragmented.	2.13	1.00	39
1-20	Lack of interoperability between financial infrastructures.	2.13	1.06	39
1-21	Limited competition.	2.28	1.17	39
1-34	Long chains of intermediaries make the passing of information between the issuer and the investor inefficient.	2.44	1.10	39
1-17	Too many levels of infrastructure which offer redundant services.	2.59	1.09	37

Table 9: Reasons for the Inefficiency of the cross-border Post-Trading System in Europe: Organization and Competition

The fact that back office costs arise for financial institutions for connecting to each of the different post-trading systems is rather agreed to [1.84] (see Table 10).

	Main reasons for inefficiency of cross-border post-trading in Europe are:	Mean	STD	n (N=40)
1-24	Back office costs arise for financial institutions for connecting to each of the different post-trading systems.	1.84	0.72	38
1-23	Too much manual intervention in some post-trading processes.	2.56	0.88	36

Table 10: Reasons for the Inefficiency of the cross-border Post-Trading System in Europe: Processes and IT

Table 11 shows deficiencies in risk management processes - as named by some participants in round 1 - are not seen as the main reasons for the inefficiency of cross-border post-trading in Europe.

	Main reasons for inefficiency of cross-border post-trading in Europe are:	Mean	STD	n (N=40)
1-27	Lack of standardization in risk management.	2.65	0.86	37
1-25	New clearing houses are not always offering an equivalent level of risk coverage and market protection as the incumbent clearing houses.	2.79	1.07	38
1-26	Fee decreases started by some players lead the post-trading industry towards higher risk.	3.42	0.92	38

Table 11: Reasons for the Inefficiency of the cross-border Post-Trading System in Europe: Risk Management

In terms of regulatory issues as causes for the inefficiency, the experts rather agree [1.92] that "European regulation is influenced by political agendas which lead to compromise-based solutions that reflect the political reality rather than the most efficient solutions" (see Table 12).

High STD (1.31) can be observed concerning the hypotheses that there is "Not enough focus of the European policy makers on efficiency". Figure 13 shows how this view differs among the relevant expert groups.

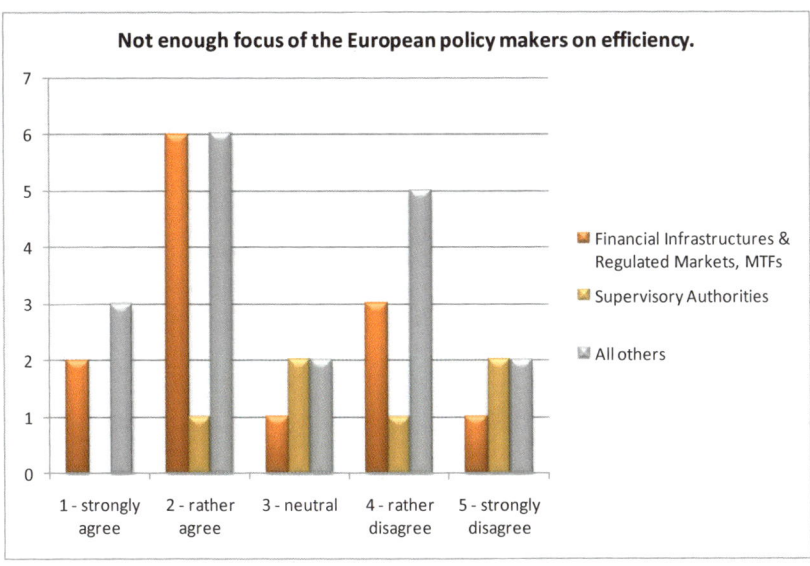

Figure 13: Distribution of Answers regarding Hypothesis 1-29

	Main reasons for inefficiency of cross-border post-trading in Europe are:	Mean	STD	n (N=40)
1-32	European regulation is influenced by political agendas which lead to compromise-based solutions that reflect the political reality rather than the most efficient solutions.	1.92	0.86	37
1-31	Pan-European regulation allows regulatory arbitrage.	2.54	0.90	37
1-28	MiFID increased the complexity of trading and post-trading.	2.71	1.09	38
1-29	Not enough focus of the European policy makers on efficiency.	2.89	1.31	37
1-30	Not enough focus of the European policy makers on safety.	3.13	1.04	38

Table 12: Reasons for the Inefficiency of the cross-border Post-Trading System in Europe: Regulation

Table 13 presents the approval rates to further hypotheses in context of the inefficiency of cross-border post-trading in Europe.

	Main reasons for inefficiency of cross-border post-trading in Europe are:	Mean	STD	n (N=40)
1-33	Financial intermediaries have more power than issuers and investors.	2.45	1.13	38
1-35	Settlement failures and the way they are treated (allowing delivery failures to go on almost endlessly).	2.74	1.07	35

Table 13: Reasons for the Inefficiency of the cross-border Post-Trading System in Europe: Other

Intermediate Summary:

In sum, the experts agree that the European post-trading system is efficient at the national level. They agree that, in the national context, the system shows high settlement rates, a high technical reliability, and financial infrastructures provide effective risk mitigation tools.

In contrast, the experts disagree with the hypothesis that the European post-trading system is efficient in case of cross-border transactions. As most important reasons for inefficiency the still existing Giovannini Barriers were identified. Moreover, the experts argue that some financial intermediaries exploiting these inefficiencies, high back office costs for financial institutions and European regulation influenced by political agendas to be main reasons for the inefficiency of cross-border post-trading in Europe.

Specific expert quotes:

One participant wonders *"why the chain [of intermediaries] still exists today despite all the harmonization work that has been carried out and is still on-going. Holding through a chain of intermediaries means adding extra layers to the relationship between the issuer of the securities and the shareholder."* Another comment claims that *"these layers are a barrier to shareholder visibility: it prevents the issuer from knowing his shareholders and entering into a dialogue with them"*.

3.5 An Ideal European Post-Trading System

The second question from the initial round of the Delphi study required the panelists to outline their notion of an ideal post-trading system for Europe.

Most consensus was reached on the hypotheses stating that an ideal European post-trading system would be characterized by the elimination of the Giovannini barriers (fiscal barriers [1.55], legal barriers [1.56], and technical and market practice barriers [1.64]), where the majority of participants agreed and very little dissent (low STD) is observable (see Table 14).

	The ideal European post-trading system would be characterized by:	Mean	STD	n (N=40)
2-09	Elimination of fiscal (Giovannini) barriers.	1.55	0.72	39
2-07	Elimination of legal (Giovannini) barriers.	1.56	0.72	39
2-08	Elimination of technical and market practice (Giovannini) barriers.	1.64	0.71	39

Table 14: Characterization of the ideal European Post-Trading System: Giovannini Barriers

"Access and interoperability in the area of trading, clearing, and settlement", "Freedom of choice for investors with regard to trading, clearing, settlement, and custody" [both 1.65] and "Competition on the trading level to keep prices low and innovation high" [1.79] all seem to be further characteristics of an ideally structured post-trading system (rather agreement with tendency towards strong agreement). The idea of extreme concentration with "Exactly one clearing house and one CSD" as possible characteristic of an ideal post-trading system for Europe faces quite strong objections: The majority of experts rather disagrees [4.03]. Instead, the experts trust that competition on the clearing level will keep prices low and innovation high [1.92] (see Table 15). There is no consensus that vertical disintegration is an ideal market organization (see Figure 14) and that there will be one domestic post-trading infrastructure (see Figure 15).

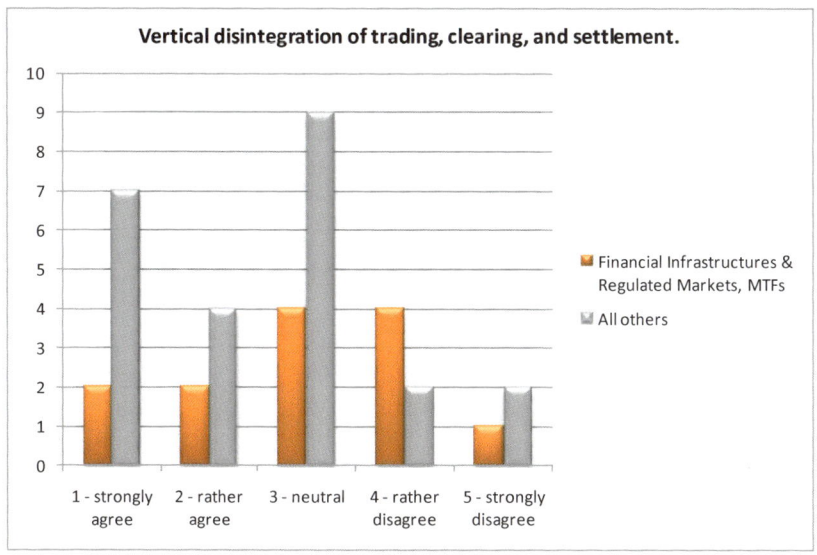

Figure 14: Distribution of Answers regarding Hypothesis 2-03

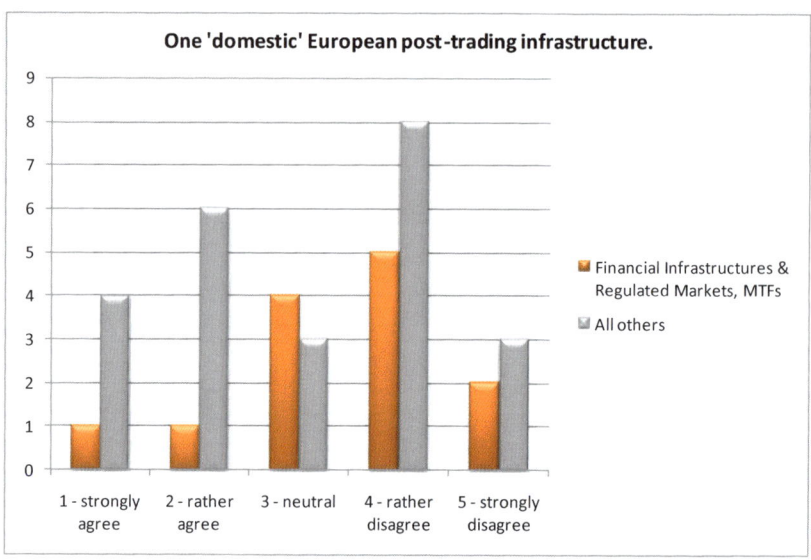

Figure 15: Distribution of Answers regarding Hypothesis 2-06

	The ideal European post-trading system would be characterized by:	Mean	STD	n (N=40)
2-04	Access and interoperability in the area of trading, clearing, and settlement.	1.65	0.72	37
2-05	Freedom of choice for investors with regard to trading, clearing, settlement, and custody.	1.65	0.86	37
2-10	Competition on the trading level to keep prices low and innovation high.	1.79	0.84	38
2-13	Competition on the clearing level to keep prices low and innovation high.	1.92	0.75	38
2-01	A system based on competition and market innovation on each layer of the value chain as existent today.	2.21	0.84	38

The Future of the European Post-Trading System 57

2-03	Vertical disintegration of trading, clearing, and settlement.	2.68	1.25	37
2-02	Decentralized financial infrastructures to avoid (systemic) risk accumulation.	2.74	0.98	38
2-06	One 'domestic' European post-trading infrastructure.	3.16	1.28	37
2-19	Exactly one clearing house and one CSD.	4.03	1.12	37

Table 15: Characterization of the ideal European Post-Trading System: Market Organization

As shown in Table 16, other aspects either implying strong market concentration such as the call for "a mandatory participation in T2S" [3.42] or far-reaching restrictions with regard to profit generation such as the proposal that "Clearing houses and CSDs operate on a not-for-profit basis or under constrained profit rules" [3.33] are also rather disagreed to by the panelists.

The experts believe that cash and securities should be integrated in one platform [2.00]. Topics such as "One European securities register (including end customers and nominees)" [2.51] or "Clearing houses and CSDs that operate on a not-for-profit basis or under constrained profit rules" are rather seen neutral [3.33], however both with a fairly high STD [1.37 and 1.35 respectively] (see Figure 16 and Figure 17).

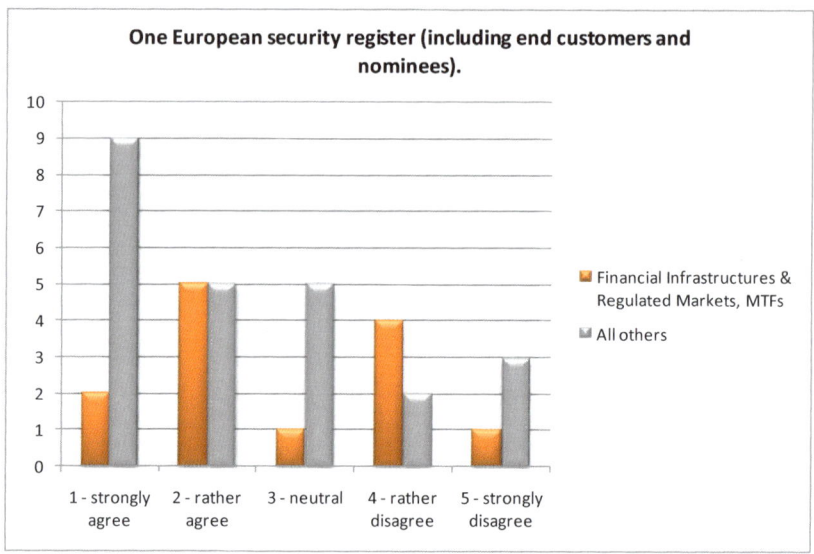

Figure 16: Distribution of Answers regarding Hypothesis 2-16

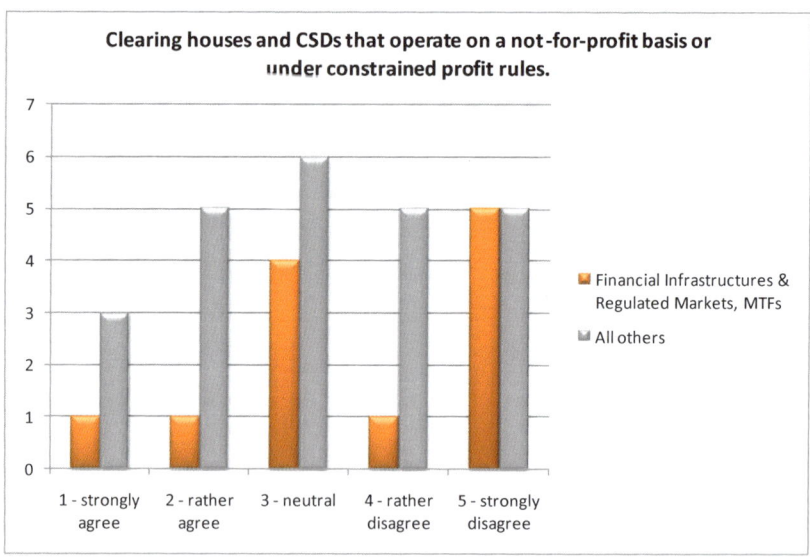

Figure 17: Distribution of Answers regarding Hypothesis 2-20

	The ideal European post-trading system would be characterized by:	Mean	STD	n (N=40)
2-18	Integration of both the cash and the securities leg in a single settlement platform.	2.00	0.97	35
2-12	Two to three clearing houses, all of which interoperable to guarantee choice of clearing venue.	2.29	0.96	38
2-14	Large clearing houses (to provide efficient netting and collateral management).	2.36	0.93	36
2-11	Clearing houses separated from exchanges.	2.38	1.04	37
2-23	Competition in asset servicing between CSDs and custodian banks to keep prices low and innovation high.	2.41	1.16	39
2-24	The ability for investors to hold assets directly in a central system.	2.46	1.00	39
2-17	Usage of central bank money for every settlement.	2.50	1.13	38
2-16	One European security register (including end customers and nominees).	2.51	1.37	37
2-15	Settlement co-location in one single settlement location.	2.57	1.19	30
2-21	T2S that is not operated by the Eurosystem.	3.18	1.09	34
2-20	Clearing houses and CSDs that operate on a not-for-profit basis or under constrained profit rules.	3.33	1.35	36

| 2-22 | A mandatory participation in T2S. | 3.42 | 1.15 | 33 |

Table 16: Characterization of the ideal European Post-Trading System: Processes and Market Infrastructure

Regarding the regulatory framework of securities trading and post-trading in Europe (see Table 17), the experts agree that an ideal regulatory framework is one that "focuses on functions rather than on institutions" [1.95] and that "distinguishes between the roles of market infrastructures and of financial entities taking credit risks" [2.00]. The majority of participants furthermore agree to the suggestion that an ideal post-trading system is characterized by an "integration of standardized OTC-products into centralized clearing" [1.97]. In this regard, consensus is apparent with the low STD of 0.85.

There is, however, low consensus on the hypotheses that the regulatory framework should "include custodian banks in the requirements applying to clearing houses and CSDs" [2.50]. This is apparent from the high STD of 1.20: Experts from financial infrastructures and regulated markets rather agree [1.85] that custodian banks should be included, while the rest of the panel is not united [2.83 with a high STD of 1.34] (see Figure 21).

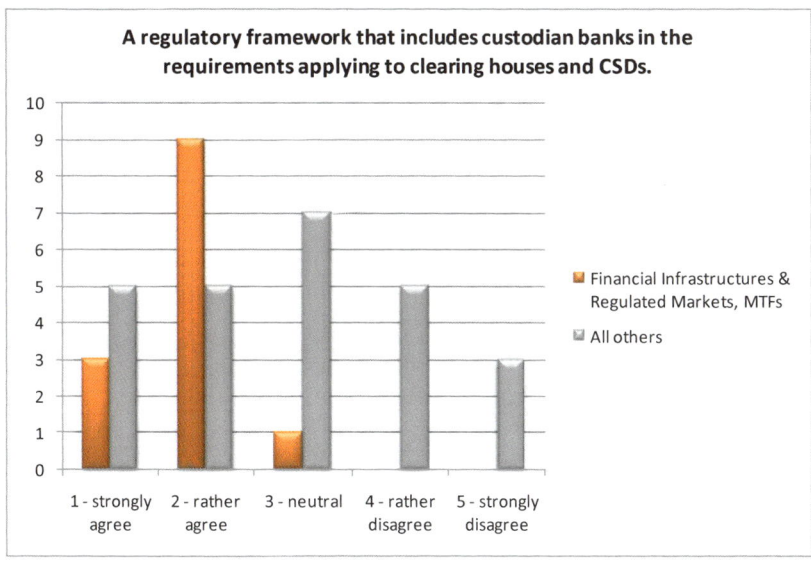

Figure 18: Distribution of Answers regarding Hypothesis 2-27

	The ideal European post-trading system would be characterized by:	Mean	STD	n (N=40)
2-25	A regulatory framework that focuses on functions rather than on institutions.	1.95	0.90	38
2-30	Standardized OTC-products integrated into centralized clearing.	1.97	0.85	38
2-26	A regulatory framework that distinguishes between the roles of market infrastructures and of financial entities taking credit risks.	2.00	0.84	38
2-28	Rules to regulate 'cherry picking' in trading and post-trading.	2.28	0.81	36
2-27	A regulatory framework that includes custodian banks in the requirements applying to clearing houses and CSDs.	2.50	1.20	38

| 2-29 | Direct access from issuer to investor. | 2.65 | 1.10 | 34 |

Table 17: Characterization of the ideal European Post-Trading System: Regulation

Intermediate Summary:

In sum, the participants characterized the ideal post-trading system as one where all Giovannini barriers have completely been eliminated and where access and interoperability warrant the freedom of choice for investors in the area of trading, clearing, and settlement. Ideally, prices are kept low and innovation high through sufficient competition, both on the trading and on the clearing level. The experts disagree that the ideal European post-trading system would feature exactly one clearing house and one CSD.

The ideal regulatory framework, according to the panelists, focuses on functions rather than on institutions and distinguishes between the roles of market infrastructures and of financial entities taking credit risks. With reference to the financial crisis, participants claim that standardized OTC-products are ideally integrated into centralized clearing; in terms of the settlement infrastructure, their preferred solution is an integration of both the cash and the securities leg within a single settlement platform.

3.6 The European Post-Trading System in the Future

The hypotheses gathered by means of the third open question describe the experts' views of how the European post-trading system is expected to look like in the year 2020. This question differs from the preceding question in that it tries to grasp a *realistic* picture of the future post-trading landscape, while question two had aimed at delivering a notion of an *idealistic* post-trading system.

This section started with the rather general statement that "European post-trading will be more integrated than today" (see Table 18). We observe articulate consensus [STD=0.51] among the panelists who rather agree to this statement with a tendency towards strong agreement [1.54].

	In 2020...	Mean	STD	n (N=40)
3-01	European post-trading will be more integrated than today.	1.54	0.51	37

Table 18: The European Post-Trading System in 2020

A series of hypotheses tackled the issue of consolidation among the players within the securities trading value chain (see Table 19). The study participants agree that the pace at which consolidation will take place will be determined not only by market forces, but also by political interventions [2.14]. Consolidation is expected to occur at all levels of the value chain: The experts agree that in 2020 the number of exchanges [2.42] and of Multilateral Trading Facilities [2.32] will be smaller than today, that "the European post-trading system will consist of two to three clearing houses" [2.50] and that "the European post-trading system will consist of less CSDs than today" [2.03]. There is also consensus that the "number of custodian banks will be smaller" [2.24]. The experts are, however, rather neutral towards the proposition that the European post-trading system "will consist of a high number of access providers to clearing and settlement institutions" [2.81]. The STD for the latter two is fairly low [0.86] and indicates strong consent. It seems worth mentioning that there is also broad consensus that "consolidation of clearing houses will take place through aggressive competition" [2.45], again with a fairly little STD [0.83].

The experts are neutral towards the suggestion that in 2020 the European post-trading system "will consist of one single settlement institution" [3.24], but with a high STD (see Figure 19).

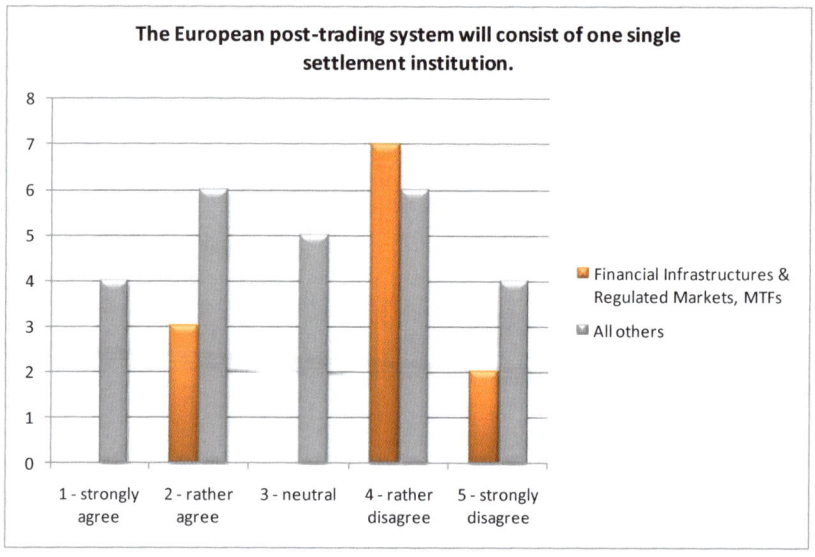

Figure 19: Distribution of Answers regarding Hypothesis 3-08

They disagree that there will be "one user-owned and user-governed settlement infrastructure" [3.61]. Also, there is rather disagreement that "the entire European post-trading system will come under the governance from regulators or central banks" [3.49] (see Figure 20).

The Future of the European Post-Trading System

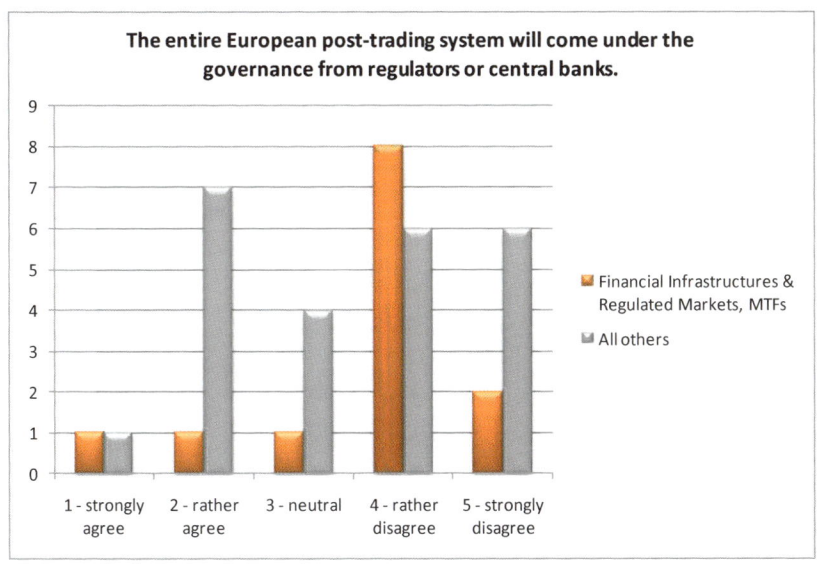

Figure 20: Distribution of Answers regarding Hypothesis 3-12

	In 2020...	Mean	STD	n (N=40)
3-07	The European post-trading system will consist of less CSDs than today.	2.03	0.90	37
3-13	The pace at which consolidation will take place will be determined not only by market forces, but also by political interventions.	2.14	0.89	37
3-09	The number of custodian banks will be smaller.	2.24	0.86	37
3-04	The number of Multilateral Trading Facilities will be smaller than today.	2.32	1.11	37
3-03	The number of exchanges will be smaller.	2.42	1.13	38

3-06	Consolidation of clearing houses will take place through aggressive competition.	2.45	0.83	38
3-05	The European post-trading system will consist of two to three clearing houses.	2.50	0.94	36
3-10	The European post-trading system will consist of a high number of access providers to clearing and settlement institutions.	2.81	0.86	36
3-08	The European post-trading system will consist of one single settlement institution.	3.24	1.30	37
3-02	There will be no single market achieved as the current global financial crisis prevents the necessary investments.	3.43	1.09	37
3-12	The entire European post-trading system will come under the governance from regulators or central banks.	3.49	1.22	37
3-11	There will be one user-owned and user-governed settlement infrastructure.	3.61	1.10	38

Table 19: The European Post-Trading System in 2020: Market Organization

The next block of hypotheses focuses on issues of corporate governance and business development of the institutions involved in the post-trading system. With regard to the governance of post-trading infrastructures, the experts are neutral towards both hypotheses "owners of post-trading infrastructures will be vertically integrated trading platforms" [3.47] and "owners of post-trading infrastructures will be financial intermediaries" [2.78]. This can be interpreted as a tendency towards user-owned instead of vertically integrated silo structures (owned by financial intermediaries instead of exchanges).

The study participants rather disagree to the proposition that "Post-trading will continue to be an area where excessive profits are achievable"; compared to round two [3.58], this opinion even reinforced in round three [3.66]. The experts rather agree that the "main competitive battle field of agents, custodian banks, and CSDs will be custody services and corporate actions" [2.00]. Moreover, custodian banks that only operate in domestic markets will be challenged in particular [1.89]. In respect to commoditization, they are neutral towards the statement that in 2020 "Settlement services will have become a standardized commodity with little room for customization and innovation" [3.17], whereas there is a tendency towards disagreement concerning the equivalent statement that relates to custody services [3.49].[5]

The remaining suggestions put up for discussion in this area seem to be rather less controversial. They are depicted in Table 20.

	In 2020...	Mean	STD	n (N=40)
3-20	Custodian banks that only serve domestic markets will be particularly challenged.	1.89	0.92	38
3-18	The main competitive battle field of agents, custodian banks, and CSDs will be custody services and corporate actions.	2.00	0.94	37
3-22	CSDs will start providing more value added services.	2.03	0.87	37

---

[5] In the second round the original question was: "Settlement and custody services will have become a standardized commodity with little room for customization and innovation" [3.35]. Due to multiple comments we divided the question into one for settlement and one for custody.

3-23	Complex institutional transactions will be niches for specialized post-trade providers.	2.19	0.91	37
3-17	Global custody will be the most profitable post-trading segment.	2.57	0.83	37
3-19	Clearing and settlement infrastructures will improve their services through cooperation rather than through competition.	2.68	0.93	38
3-15	The owners of post-trading infrastructures will be financial intermediaries.	2.78	0.76	36
3-21	Settlement services will have become a standardized commodity with little room for customization and innovation.	3.17	1.00	36
3-14	The owners of post-trading infrastructures will be vertically integrated trading platforms.	3.47	0.81	36
3-48	Custody services will have become a standardized commodity with little room for customization and innovation.	3.49	0.89	35
3-16	Post-trading will continue to be an area where excessive profits are achievable.	3.66	1.10	38

Table 20: The European Post-Trading System in 2020: Governance and Business Development

Numerous opinions were given in round one in respect to T2S, the Eurosystem's platform that intends to make settlements across national borders simpler and more cost-efficient (see Table 21). Apparently, there is consensus among the majority of the panel that T2S will be up and running in 2020 [1.75]. The experts also believe that "the launch of T2S will speed up the European consolidation process" [1.89], "will contribute to a borderless and seamless European post-trading system" [2.22], and that by 2020, "T2S will have reduced the costs of cross-border trade settlement" [2.25]. Not unexpectedly, the latter hypothesis is especially supported by the experts from the "Supervisory Authorities" group, but also by the some representatives from "Financial Infrastructures" (see Figure 21). Moreover, there is no consensus regarding the following hypotheses: "T2S will maintain the efficiency of domestic trade settlement" (STD=1.29, see Figure 22) and "T2S will have blurred the differences between CSDs and custodian banks" (STD=1.21, see Figure 23).

However, the participants are neutral toward the suggestion that the "overall cost of clearing and settlement will not reduce after T2S because CSDs will still provide custody and corporate action processing (and will retain settlement information in their systems)" [3.11].

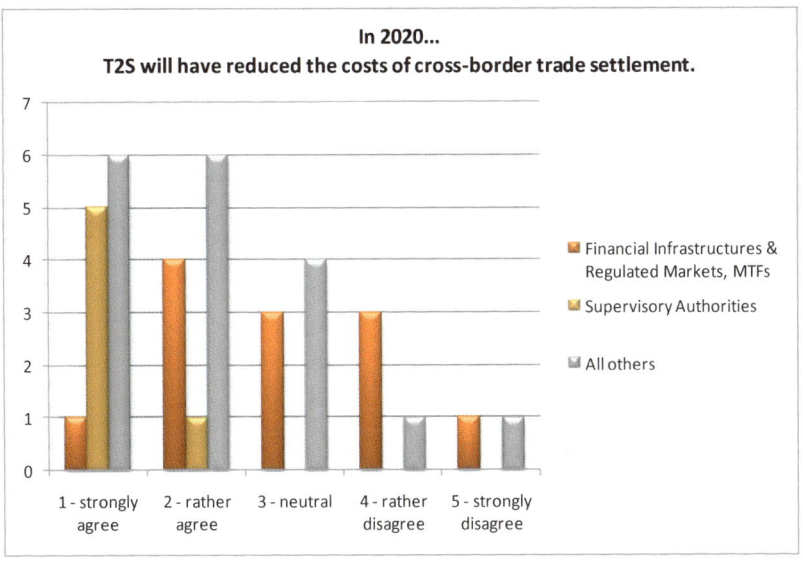

Figure 21: Distribution of Answers regarding Hypothesis 3-28

The Future of the European Post-Trading System

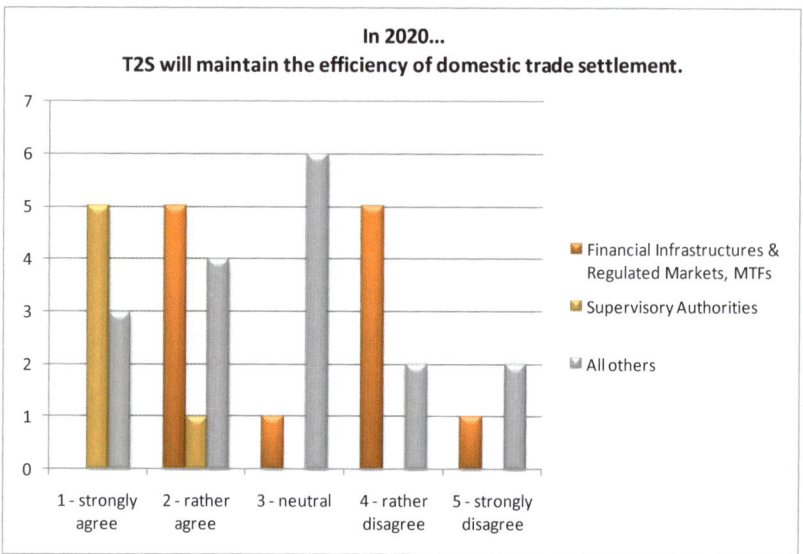

Figure 22: Distribution of Answers regarding Hypothesis 3-29

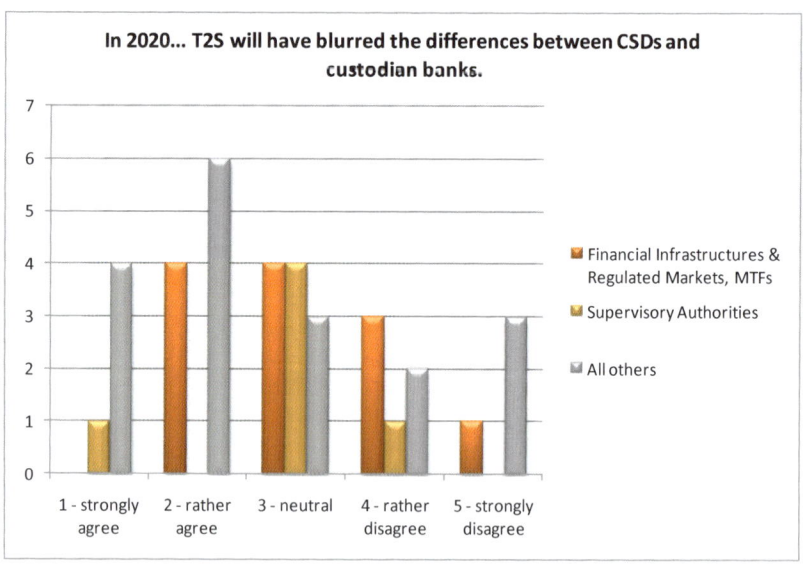

Figure 23: Distribution of Answers regarding Hypothesis 3-27

The Future of the European Post-Trading System

	In 2020...	Mean	STD	n (N=40)
3-24	T2S will be live.	1.75	0.77	36
3-26	The launch of T2S will speed up the European consolidation process.	1.89	1.01	36
3-33	T2S will contribute to a borderless and seamless European post-trading system.	2.22	1.05	36
3-28	T2S will have reduced the costs of cross-border trade settlement.	2.25	1.20	36
3-34	Collateral Central Bank Management (CCBM2) will contribute to a borderless and seamless European post-trading system.	2.26	0.78	35
3-32	CSDs will use the same underlying IT infrastructures: T2S for settlement and private infrastructures for the other services.	2.37	0.65	35
3-25	T2S will start off as a provider of settlement-only functions but will add on other functions as it develops.	2.58	1.16	36
3-30	T2S will have led to a legal and fiscal harmonization in Europe.	2.63	1.14	35
3-29	T2S will maintain the efficiency of domestic trade settlement.	2.63	1.29	35
3-27	T2S will have blurred the differences between CSDs and custodian banks.	2.83	1.21	36

		Mean	STD	n
3-31	The overall cost of clearing and settlement will not reduce after T2S because CSDs will still provide custody and corporate action processing (and will retain settlement information in their systems).	3.11	1.06	36

Table 21: The European Post-Trading System in 2020: TARGET2-Securities

A multitude of suggestions were brought up in the first round of this Delphi study on how the European post-trading system is expected to look like in the year 2020 with regard to its regulatory framework (see Table 22). Again, the Giovannini barriers were subject of these suggestions: The participants concur in that technical and market practice barriers will be eliminated in 2020 [2.16 and 2.26 respectively]. Concerning the elimination of legal barriers, the experts are neutral [2.92], whereas regarding the elimination of fiscal barriers until 2020, they rather disagree [3.53].

	In 2020...	Mean	STD	n (N=40)
3-35	The technical (Giovannini) barriers will be eliminated.	2.16	0.97	38
3-36	The market practice (Giovannini) barriers will be eliminated.	2.26	0.95	38
3-37	The legal (Giovannini) barriers will be eliminated.	2.92	1.05	38
3-38	The fiscal (Giovannini) barriers will be eliminated.	3.53	0.89	38

Table 22: The European Post-Trading System in 2020: Giovannini Barriers

As shown in Table 23, the experts expect the CSDs to create networks offering single access to clients [1.89] and European clearing houses providing services for complex financial products [1.95]. Moreover, they are optimistic towards the implementation of the European Code of Conduct for Clearing and Settlement as they agree that price transparency in clearing and settlement [2.11], access and interoperability [2.14], and services unbundling and account separation of clearing and settlement [2.22] will be implemented in 2020.

	In 2020...	Mean	STD	n (N=40)
3-45	CSDs will create networks offering single access to clients.	1.89	0.70	37
3-44	European clearing houses will provide services for complex financial products (like CDS).	1.95	0.81	37
3-39	Price transparency of clearing and settlement will be implemented.	2.11	1.02	37
3-40	Access and interoperability of clearing and settlement will be implemented.	2.14	0.95	37
3-41	Service unbundling and account separation of clearing and settlement will be implemented.	2.22	1.03	37
3-42	There will be an EU-wide regulation of post-trading.	2.38	0.98	37
3-43	European clearing houses will be supervised by a central European supervisory authority rather than by national authorities.	2.57	1.14	37
3-46	The integration between European and US post-trading infrastructures will be established.	3.16	1.05	38
3-47	The integration between European and Asian post-trading infrastructures will be established.	3.45	1.03	38

Table 23: The European Post-Trading System in 2020: Integration

Intermediate Summary:

The experts assume that the European post-trading landscape will be more integrated in 2020 than it is today. In this environment, custodian banks that only serve domestic markets will be challenged. The main competitive battle field of agents, custodian banks, and CSDs will be custody services and corporate actions. Initiatives set off today will be finalized in 2020, such as the implementation of T2S that will speed up the European consolidation process. CSDs are expected to create networks offering single access to clients and European clearing houses will provide services for complex products (like CDS).

3.7 Measures to Improve the European Post-Trading System

The fourth question from the first round of the Delphi study asked the panelists to outline measures for improvement of the European post-trading system.

The experts overall are neutral towards the first hypothesis "There is no need for action: Financial infrastructures have been very robust in the financial crisis" [3.18]. Only single experts have extreme controversial opinions: Three experts fully agreed to this statement while two strongly disagreed (see Table 24).

	Measures to improve the post-trading system in context of the financial crisis are:	Mean	STD	n (N=40)
4-01	There is no need for action: Financial infrastructures have been very robust in the financial crisis.	3.18	1.17	39

Table 24: Measures to improve the Post-Trading System in Context of the financial Crisis

The first block of hypotheses addresses general measures for the improvement of the post-trading system (see Table 25). The experts rather agreed that the focus should be on the soundness of the post-trading system [2.24] and on reducing the system's dependence on banks [2.33] in view of the fragility they have demonstrated during the financial crisis.

	Measures to improve the post-trading system in context of the financial crisis are:	Mean	STD	n (N=40)
4-02	Focus on the soundness of the post-trading system.	2.24	0.97	38
4-03	Reduce the system's dependence on banks in view of the fragility they have demonstrated (some financial conglomerates are too big to fail).	2.33	0.93	39
4-04	Consolidation of financial infrastructures.	2.64	1.01	39

Table 25: Measures to improve the Post-Trading System in Context of the financial Crisis: Organization

The next hypotheses, which focus on measures for improvement in the area of infrastructures, are mainly rather agreed to by the experts. Especially establishing interoperability of clearing houses and CSDs finds strong support [1.89]. Clearing houses in particular should stay neutral and should not be dependent on single financial institutions [1.95]. Moreover, the experts rather agree that the separation of financial infrastructures and intermediaries should be maintained [2.18].

The experts also rather agree that the traceability of securities needs to be improved [2.11], that Collateral Central Bank Management (CCBM2) – a new single platform for the management of Eurosystem collateral – will improve liquidity and collateral management in the euro zone [2.12], and that OTC derivatives should be integrated into a centralized clearing house [2.21]. The experts are neutral towards the propositions of "introducing a central post-trading infrastructure to maximize economies of scale" or of "introducing T2S to improve liquidity and collateral management in the euro zone" as measures to improve the post-trading system.

The experts rather agree that risk aspects should be considered for management compensations of the post-trade industry [2.38].

	Measures to improve the post-trading system in context of the financial crisis are:	Mean	STD	n (N=40)
4-08	Establish interoperability solutions between and among clearing houses and CSDs.	1.89	0.86	38
4-07	Ensure neutrality of clearing houses (no dependence on a single financial institution).	1.95	0.87	38
4-12	Improve the traceability of securities (e.g. outstanding deliveries and settled instructions).	2.11	1.01	38
4-11	Introduction of CCBM2 to improve liquidity and collateral management in the euro zone.	2.12	0.88	34
4-05	Maintain the separation of different roles of financial infrastructures and intermediaries.	2.18	0.73	38
4-13	Integration of OTC derivatives into a centralized clearing house.	2.21	0.99	38
4-06	Consideration of risk aspects in the management compensations of the post-trading industry.	2.38	1.09	37
4-10	Introduction of T2S to improve liquidity and collateral management in the euro zone.	2.51	1.17	35
4-09	Introduction of a central post-trading infrastructure to maximize economies of scale.	3.16	1.07	37

Table 26: Measures to improve the Post-Trading System in Context of the financial Crisis: Infrastructures

The next group of hypotheses addresses risk issues (see Table 27). The agreement is strongest [1.63] for the proposition that financial infrastructures should focus on providing safe and secure services. The experts also rather agree that there should be a stronger cooperation between the post-trading industry and the issuers of innovative products to improve risk management [1.92]. They rather agree that financial infrastructures should increase their operational risk management [2.08], that the usage of central bank money should be increased [2.11], that the collateral and margining rules should be harmonized [2.16], and that the time of post-trade processing should be reduced [2.24].

	Measures to improve the post-trading system in context of the financial crisis are:	Mean	STD	n (N=40)
4-16	Financial infrastructures should focus on providing safe and secure services (concerning settlement/delivery, counterparty, and default).	1.63	0.75	38
4-15	Stronger cooperation between the post-trading industry and the issuers of innovative products to improve risk management.	1.92	0.80	37
4-20	Financial infrastructures should increase operational risk management.	2.08	0.84	39
4-18	Increased use of central bank money.	2.11	0.73	38
4-19	Harmonization of collateral and margining rules.	2.16	1.03	38
4-17	Reduction of post-trade processing time.	2.24	1.00	38
4-14	Ensure diversification of clearing houses in terms of customer groups and products.	2.74	0.95	38

Table 27: Measures to improve the Post-Trading System in Context of the financial Crisis: Risk

In the next step, the participants of the study evaluate two hypotheses focusing on IT issues (see Table 28). They rather agree that financial infrastructures should ensure to cope with the rapid increase of volumes expected in times of a crisis [1.92]. The hypothesis that financial infrastructures should operate in a near real-time mode so that users always have a near- time view of their positions receives a mean of [2.03].

	Measures to improve the post-trading system in context of the financial crisis are:	Mean	STD	n (N=40)
4-21	Financial infrastructures should ensure to cope with the rapid increase in volumes expected in times of a crisis.	1.92	0.88	38
4-22	Financial infrastructures should operate in a near real-time mode so that users always have a near real-time view of their positions.	2.03	1.00	38

Table 28: Measures to improve the Post-Trading System in Context of the financial Crisis: IT

The next block of hypotheses addresses regulatory issues (see Table 29). Interestingly, one hypothesis finds solid backing: The experts strongly support the proposal that the regulation of rating agencies should be improved [1.43] with a high level of consent as can be seen from the low STD of only 0.60. A number of other hypotheses are welcomed by the study participants as measures to improve the post-trading system: The experts claim that supervisory bodies should use a consistent set of standards and should communicate openly with each other [1.66]; they agree that it is necessary to improve the transparency of complex financial products such as mortgages and CDS [1.68]; and that competition and a level playing field for providers of securities services are to be promoted [1.74]. Moreover, they rather agree that legal barriers should be eliminated [1.84] and that near-time transparency of

OTC derivatives trades for regulators is an important measure [1.92]. Finally, they concur that clearing houses' defaulting procedures and the underlying legal framework should be harmonized [1.92].

	Measures to improve the post-trading system in context of the financial crisis are:	Mean	STD	n (N=40)
4-35	Improve regulation of rating agencies.	1.43	0.60	37
4-32	Supervisory bodies should use a consistent set of standards and should communicate openly with each other.	1.66	0.67	38
4-31	Improve transparency of complex financial products (e.g. mortgages and CDS).	1.68	0.70	38
4-26	Maintain / foster competition and a level playing field for providers of securities services.	1.74	0.55	38
4-23	Elimination of legal (GiovanninI) barriers.	1.84	0.89	38
4-30	Near-time transparency of OTC derivatives trades for regulators.	1.92	0.73	38
4-34	Harmonization of the clearing houses' defaulting procedures and the underlying legal framework.	1.92	0.97	38
4-33	Review systemically relevant functions (e.g. through market share or functionality such as high volume internalization) with a view to applying consistent regulation.	2.03	0.76	37

4-29	Intervention of authorities to improve efficiency if the markets do not make enough progress (e.g. in context of the European Code of Conduct for Clearing and Settlement).	2.50	1.03	38
4-25	Avoid competition between clearing houses in terms of risk management by regulation / supervision.	2.54	1.10	37
4-27	A directive can be a driver for an efficient single European market.	2.63	1.13	38
4-24	Avoid competition between clearing houses in terms of risk management by voluntary industry agreement.	2.73	0.96	37
4-28	Extended MiFID to post-trading services.	3.43	1.17	37

Table 29: Measures to improve the Post-Trading System in Context of the financial Crisis: Regulation

Intermediate Summary:

In summary, the Delphi study panelists agreed on quite a number of measures capable of improving the post-trading system: In terms of infrastructures, they accentuated that interoperability solutions between and among clearing houses and CSDs should be established and that neutrality of clearing houses shall be ensured. In terms of risk, financial infrastructures should focus on providing safe and secure services and stronger cooperation between the post-trading industry and the issuers of innovative products should be put in place to improve risk management. At the same time financial infrastructures should ensure to cope with the rapid increase in volumes expected in times of a crisis.

The supervisory bodies are expected to use a consistent set of standards and to communicate openly with each other. The participants expect a regulatory environment that fosters competition and a level playing field for providers of securities services. They furthermore call for an improvement of the regulation of rating agencies in conjunction with an improvement of the transparency of complex financial products. The elimination of legal (Giovannini) barriers, a near-time transparency of OTC derivatives trades for regulators and the harmonization of the clearing houses' defaulting procedures and the underlying legal framework are seen as further measures to improve the post-trading system in the context of the financial crisis.

Specific expert quotes:

One expert emphasizes that "*an initiative like T2S should not become a bureaucracy, but must keep clear customer focus. Some kind of reward model for improving efficiency in the post-trade arena must be considered, in order to keep entrepreneurial spirit and innovation capacity alive for the future*".

In terms of the harmonization of the clearing houses' defaulting procedures and the underlying legal framework, one participant gave voice to his concern that "*if a directive were to be issued, then it should be detailing the framework, regulatory requirements and the operating principles only, but not the way in which the business is being conducted. This would kill innovation.*"

3.8 Risk Management Issues of the European Post-Trading System

The fifth question from the initial round of the Delphi study asked the panelists to outline the most important risk management issues the post-trading-system needs to cope with.

The experts were confronted in round two with a proposition that can – in light of the financial crisis – be understood as controversial: "There is no need for action: The current financial infrastructure is very stable". While the panel overall rather disagrees with a tendency towards neutrality [3.57], we gain interesting insights when looking at the different expert groups individually: The participants from financial infrastructures and regulated markets are rather neutral [2.92] whereas all other experts do see the need for action in the area of risk management issues [3.90] (see Figure 24 and Table 30).

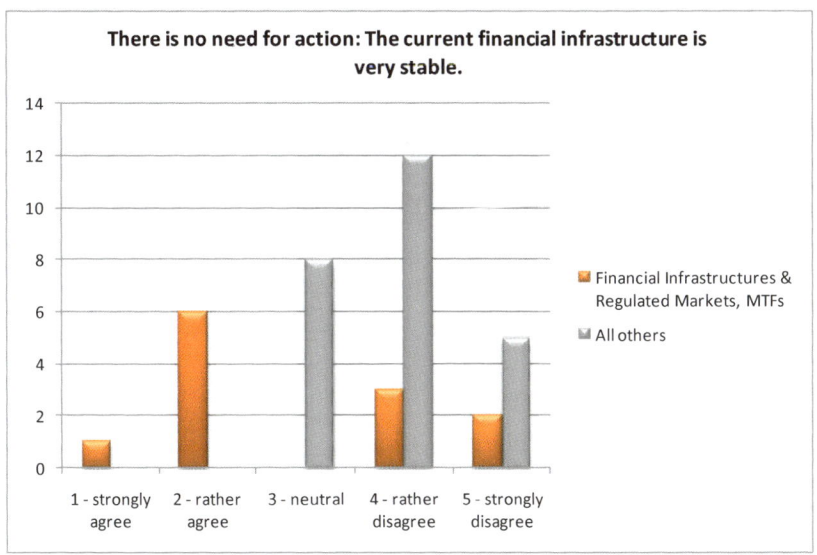

Figure 24: Distribution of Answers regarding Hypothesis 5-01

	The most important risk management issues the post-trading system needs to cope with are:	Mean	STD	n (N=40)
5-01	There is no need for action: The current financial infrastructure is very stable.	3.57	1.07	37

Table 30: Most important Risk Management Issues the Post-Trading System needs to cope with

The experts rather agree (with tendency towards strong agreement) [1.61] that one of the most important issues is transparency: all financial institutions and infrastructures need to be able to identify their customers, their counterparties and the instruments they have invested in (see Table 30).

	The most important risk management issues the post-trading system needs to cope with are:	Mean	STD	n (N=40)
5-04	Transparency (financial institutions and infrastructures need to be able to identify their customer, their counterparty, and the instrument they have invested in).	1.61	0.72	38
5-03	There is a risk that competition and innovation are at the expense of safety.	2.45	1.11	38
5-02	Fee reductions not based on efficiency improvements are a danger.	2.70	1.02	37

Table 31: Most important Risk Management Issues the Post-Trading System needs to cope with: General Statements

The experts rather agree that another important issue the post-trading system has to deal with is the enhancement of the financial institutions' collateral management [1.92]. Moreover, they emphasize the importance of implementing highly secured processes [2.00] (see Table 32).

	The most important risk management issues the post-trading system needs to cope with are:	Mean	STD	n (N=40)
5-09	Optimizing financial institutions' collateral management.	1.92	0.65	36
5-07	Implementation of highly secured processes as promoted by CPSS-IOSCO or by ESCB and CESR.	2.00	0.85	34
5-08	Elimination of settlement risks by increasing the usage of central bank money.	2.22	0.82	37
5-05	Change management of the large number of infrastructure reform projects.	2.44	0.70	34
5-06	Separation of notary function and financial services provided by CSDs (notary function should not be put at risk).	2.54	1.07	35
5-10	Riskier derivatives need to be settled on a trade-by-trade basis, not in a netting system.	3.12	1.19	33

Table 32: Most important Risk Management Issues the Post-Trading System needs to cope with: Organization

There is strong consent regarding the following theses: The experts agree that CSDs are exposed to operational risk and should therefore ensure state-of-the-art operational resilience [1.61]. Timely clearing and settlement including the related reporting are also seen as important risk issues [1.71] (see Table 33).

	The most important risk management issues the post-trading system needs to cope with are:	Mean	STD	n (N=40)
5-13	CSDs are exposed to operational risk events and should therefore ensure state-of-the-art operational resilience.	1.61	0.64	38
5-12	Financial institutions and intermediaries need timely clearing and settlement including related reports to determine risks and account positions precisely.	1.71	0.52	38
5-11	Risk evaluation of illiquid securities (due to the divergence between fundamental value and market value).	2.11	0.77	37

Table 33: Most important Risk Management Issues the Post-Trading System needs to cope with: Risk

The experts strongly agree that it is important to harmonize legal certainty [1.47] and to standardize the rules of finality, default procedures, and cancellation rules [1.43]. They rather agree with tendency towards strong agreement that the implementation of the Settlement Finality Directive and the Financial Collateral Directive [1.59] as well as stability of the legal and regulatory environment [1.55] are further important issues concerning risk management in the post-trading industry (see Table 34).

	The most important risk management issues the post-trading system needs to cope with are:	Mean	STD	n (N=40)
5-15	Harmonization of rules of finality, default procedures, and cancellation rules.	1.43	0.50	37
5-14	Harmonization of legal certainty.	1.47	0.60	38
5-17	Stability of the legal and regulatory environment.	1.55	0.60	38
5-16	Implementation of the Settlement Finality Directive and Financial Collateral Directive.	1.59	0.86	34
5-19	Establish a fast reacting international task force in case of failure of systemically relevant market infrastructures.	2.14	1.02	36
5-18	Prevent financial infrastructures from taking too much credit risk (when competing with financial institutions) by regulation.	2.22	0.93	36

Table 34: Most important Risk Management Issues the Post-Trading System needs to cope with: Regulation

Finally, the experts rather agree that the introduction of clearing houses for OTC derivatives is an important issue [1.78] as well as the monitoring of the risk of the defaulting of derivatives issuers [1.84] (see Table 35).

	The most important risk management issues the post-trading system needs to cope with are:	Mean	STD	n (N=40)
5-22	Introduction of clearing houses for OTC-traded derivatives.	1.78	0.58	37
5-23	Monitor the risk of derivatives issuers defaulting.	1.84	0.76	37
5-21	Enhancement of linked settlement of OTC-traded equities.	2.31	0.82	36
5-20	Regulate OTC markets by similar rules as regulated markets.	2.62	1.16	37

Table 35: Most important Risk Management Issues the Post-Trading System needs to cope with: Derivatives

Intermediate Summary:

In sum, the experts emphasize the importance of harmonization in the area of risk management. They stress out the need for state-of-the-art operational resilience for CSDs and the importance of timely clearing and settlement (including related reporting). Moreover, legal certainty, rules of finality, default procedures, and cancellation rules and the stability of the legal and regulatory environment were named in context of risk mitigation. The experts see the need for more transparency, for the introduction of clearing houses for OTC-traded derivatives, and for monitoring the defaulting risk of derivatives issuers. Furthermore, optimizing financial institutions' collateral management and the implementation of highly secured processes as promoted by CPSS-IOSCO or by ESCB and CESR as well as the Implementation of the Settlement Finality Directive and Financial Collateral Directive are agreed by the experts as the most important risk management issues the post-trading system needs to cope with.

Specific expert quotes:

One expert states that "*Financial services are global, not multi-national. Most other products and services sold around the world are multi-national, but not global. A share of stock in Paris has different rights, a different meaning, than a share of stock issued in Buenos Aires. For reasons like this, there is no one solution for regulating the banks, brokers and stock exchanges in every country. Any system that settles global trades has to be prepared to look at risk in an entirely new way*".

Another participant adds: "*Let regulators focus on the overall framework and regulatory oversight, not on the nitty gritty details. That is specialists work and there aren't many of them – with all due respect*", he concludes, "*certainly not in the European Parliament*".

3.9 IT/IS Issues of the European Post-Trading System

The hypotheses gathered by means of the last open question describe the experts' views on the most important IT/ IS issues the post-trading system has to cope with.

Most experts rather disagree [3.78] that IT-systems are not a competitive factor in the post-trading landscape anymore (see Table 36). Only three experts rather agree to this thesis. The rest of the panel believes that IT-systems are still a competitive factor in the post-trading industry. Risk due to the concentration in the post-trade industry does not seem to be an IT issue as the majority of the experts are neutral towards this proposition [2.95].

	The most important IT/ IS issues the post-trading system needs to cope with are:	Mean	STD	n (N=40)
6-01	IT-systems are not a competitive factor in the post-trading landscape anymore.	3.78	0.89	37
6-02	Risk due to the concentration in the post-trading industry.	2.95	0.78	37

Table 36: Most important IT/IS Issues the Post-Trading System needs to cope with: General Statements

Important IT issues in post-trading are the establishment of links from legacy systems to T2S and CCBM2 [2.12], the consolidation of IT platforms [2.12], and the increasing IT investments due to the dynamics in the post-trading markets [2.11]. The experts are afraid that these projects might lead to a scarcity of resources when IT-systems need to be upgraded in all parts of the post-trading area at the same time [2.03] (see Table 37).

	The most important IT/ IS issues the post-trading system needs to cope with are:	Mean	STD	n (N=40)
6-05	Scarcity of resources (staff and IT) when IT-systems need to be upgraded in all parts of the post-trading area at the same time (e.g. due to T2S).	2.03	0.87	34
6-04	Increasing IT investments due to dynamics on post-trading markets.	2.11	0.84	37
6-06	Consolidation of IT platforms.	2.12	0.77	34
6-03	To establish links from legacy systems to T2S and CCBM2.	2.12	0.98	34

Table 37: Most important IT/IS Issues the Post-Trading System needs to cope with: IT Projects

Experts rather agree with tendency towards strong agreement that IT-systems in the post-trading industry need to achieve a real STP environment to keep manual intervention low [1.72]. Further important requirements are flexibility and modularity to meet new requirements [1.83]. Achieving access and interoperability analog to the European Code of Conduct for Clearing and Settlement is also an important IT/IS issue [1.89] (see Table 38).

	The most important IT/ IS issues the post-trading system needs to cope with are:	Mean	STD	n (N=40)
6-12	IT-systems need to achieve a real STP environment in order to reduce manual intervention.	1.72	0.61	36
6-08	Flexibility / modularity of systems to meet new regulatory and product-related requirements.	1.83	0.51	36
6-13	Access and Interoperability (analog to the Code of Conduct).	1.89	0.82	36
6-09	Scalability (capacity to deal with peak volumes).	2.08	0.77	36
6-07	Availability.	2.51	0.98	35
6-10	Outsourcing of IT infrastructure (or services).	2.63	1.00	35
6-11	Outsourcing of IT infrastructure (or services) outside the EU.	3.09	0.95	35

Table 38: Most important IT/IS Issues the Post-Trading System needs to cope with: IT-system Provisioning

The harmonization of protocols and communication standards is another important IT issue [1.69]: Examples are the implementation of SWIFT / ISO[6] [2.26] and the establishment of secure internet connectivity for messaging [2.39] (see Table 39).

---

[6] In questions 6-15 and 6-16 we added "*and implementation*" in round three according to the comments from the participants. The following answers only changed marginally.

	The most important IT/ IS issues the post-trading system needs to cope with are:	Mean	STD	n (N=40)
6-14	Harmonization of protocols and communication standards.	1.69	0.82	36
6-16	Establishment *and implementation* of SWIFT / ISO as standard for messaging.	2.26	0.85	35
6-18	Establishment of secure internet connectivity for messaging.	2.39	1.02	36
6-15	Establishment *and implementation* of FIX as standard for messaging.	3.09	1.15	32
6-17	Availability of old message formats for user convenience.	3.37	0.97	35

Table 39: Most important IT/IS Issues the Post-Trading System needs to cope with: Communication

Other important IT/IS issues in post-trading that the experts emphasize are: the need for real-time or event-triggered risk management [1.84] and the interaction between clearing houses and customers and between linked clearing houses [1.89] (see Table 40).

	The most important IT/ IS issues the post-trading system needs to cope with are:	Mean	STD	n (N=40)
6-19	Real-time or event-triggered risk management.	1.84	0.76	37
6-20	Interaction between clearing houses and customers (for margin payments or collateral provision) and between linked clearing houses.	1.89	0.67	36

Table 40: Most important IT/IS Issues the Post-Trading System needs to cope with: Other

Intermediate Summary:

Important IT/IS issues in post-trading are are the flexibility of the systems to meet the new regulatory and product-related requirements, the harmonization of protocols and communication standards, and the access to and interoperability of the systems. Moreover, IT-systems need to achieve real STP environments in order to reduce manual interventions.

Further requirements concerning IT in post-trading are real-time or event-triggered risk management and the interactions between clearing houses and customers and between linked clearing houses due to new market situations such as competitive clearing, which changes the processes in this area essentially.

Specific expert quotes:

One of the panelists bemoans the "*avalanche of regulatory changes [that] has spurred a lot of mandatory IT work*", claiming that "*not all of it is productive, as regulators are not always able to deal with the mass of data they require*". He adds that a "*major issue that has come up with MiFID and the Lehman default is that the local legal frameworks [are] often organized along different lines in different countries*". He states that "*as long as politicians do not take this up seriously and prefer their local influence over and above a true European community, it will remain very difficult to achieve a true single European market*".

4 Summary of Results and Outlook

The European securities post-trading system as a whole is an extremely complex network structure that has grown to today's configuration over decades. It developed at first along national boundaries. Only recently, consciousness has intensified that the concept of cross-border is on the verge of disappearing in an economy characterized by free movement of capital, work and goods, a common currency and more and more common policy and regulation.

Figure 25 gives a brief overview of important milestones and projects affecting the post-trading industry.

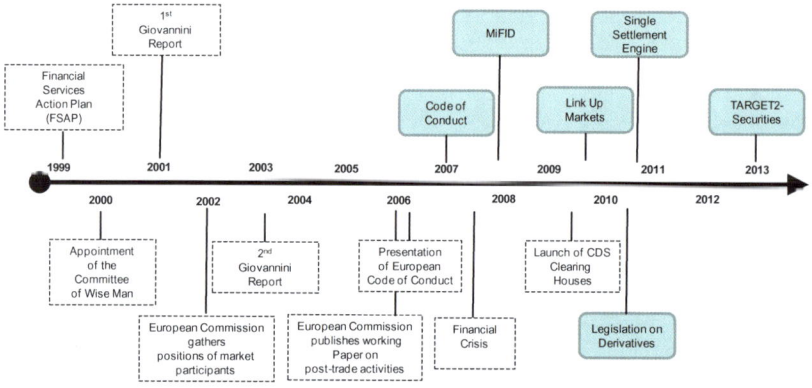

Figure 25: Milestones and Projects in the Post-Trading Industry

As one of the participants of our study puts it: "*The current complexity of post-trading across Europe is a major risk for the development of financial markets in Europe. It is far easier for local participants to invest in the US than in a number of other European countries. If the Commission wants their efforts of making Europe the most efficient knowledge-based economy in the world [to be successful], they will need to tackle the narrow minded national interests that are at stake*".

Yet, the post-trading industry seems to lack a clear vision of the preferred end-state. We took this as an opportunity to involve a number of subject-matter experts in developing a joint and coherent view of the future shape of the European post-trading system, taking into consideration the current challenges arising from the ongoing financial crisis. Post-trading issues are frequently and far too much being looked at through the eyes of infrastructures and financial intermediaries. One expert notes that "*banks and central banks as intermediaries normally have more buyer power than issuers and investors [which are] therefore sometimes disfavored*". The key positions taken, for instance, by the company that issues the securities or the investor who trades the same are often ignored. Therefore, we made an effort to include a broad majority of opinion leaders and stakeholders in this dialogue.

The discussion was fruitful and 40 experts from 158 we initially contacted participated in the final round of the Delphi study. They represented financial infrastructures, exchanges and MTFs, custodian banks and users, regulatory authorities, consultancies and technical infrastructures, academics and researchers, and associations (which include issuers and investors).

The following Figure 26 outlines the approach taken in this Delphi study. Our objective was to develop a coherent and well-grounded picture of the future state of the European post-trading system both concerning an *ideal post-trading system* and a realistic view on the *post-trading system in the future*. Starting from the participants' assessment of *today's post-trading system* and taking into consideration exogenous factors such as the *financial crisis, globalization, and competition*, we intended to identify *measures for improvement* of the post-trading system and to dispose of the industry's current inefficiencies. We realized that these measures can broadly be categorized into three interlocking areas, namely *risk management, regulation, and IT/IS*.

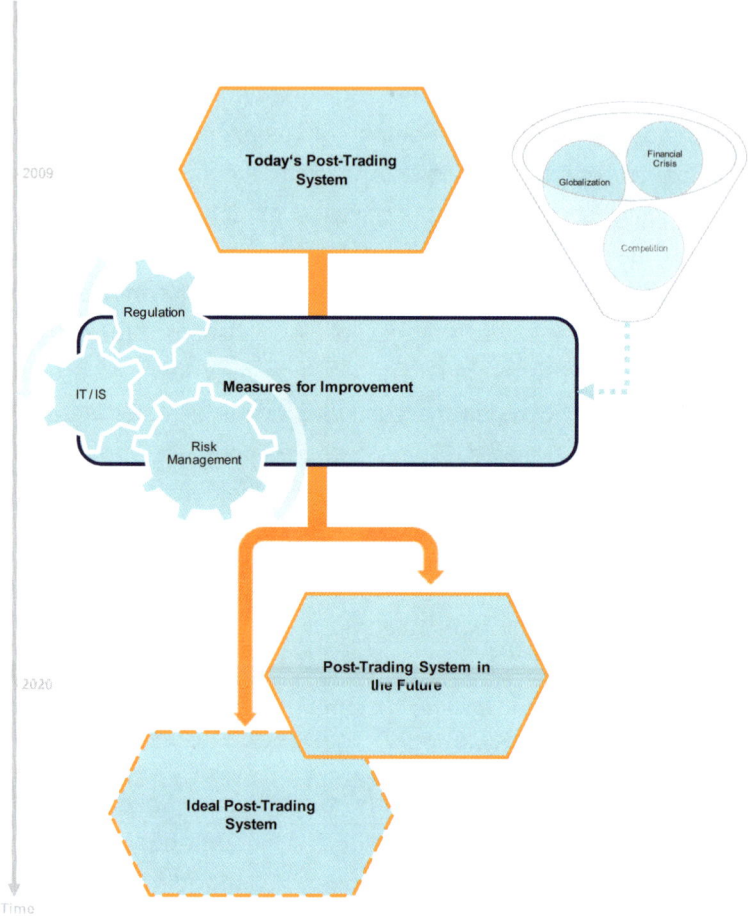

Figure 26: The Way towards a future European Post-Trading System

The assessment of **today's post-trading system** by the Delphi study expert panel turned out to be dichotomous: On the one hand, Europe's post-trading system is regarded efficient at the national level, for reasons such as high settlement rates, technical reliability and effective risk mitigation tools provided by financial infrastructures. On the other hand, the experts judge the European post-trading system to be rather inefficient at the cross-border level. The remaining Giovannini Barriers are mentioned as the main reasons for the inefficiency of cross-border transactions. In this context, the experts also criticize that some financial intermediaries and infrastructures generate revenues from the inefficiencies and that high back office costs arise for financial institutions. When it comes to evaluating the pan-European regulatory framework of securities markets, the participants of our study agree that European regulation is influenced by political agendas which lead to compromise-based solutions that reflect the political reality rather than the most efficient solutions. In sum, the experts stated that – in particular in light of the global crisis – the financial infrastructures have been very robust during the crisis. Still, a number of areas of improvement remain.

We therefore asked the experts from practice and academia to outline in a first step their view of an **"ideal" European post-trading system** and in a second step what measures need to be taken to achieve that objective. Not surprisingly, the participants characterized such an ideal post-trading system as one where all Giovannini barriers have completely been eliminated and where access and interoperability warrant the freedom of choice for investors in the area of trading, clearing, and settlement. Ideally, prices are kept low and innovation high through sufficient competition, both on the trading and on the clearing level. The experts disagree that the ideal European post-trading system would feature exactly one clearing house and one CSD. The ideal regulatory framework, according to the panelists, focuses on functions rather than on institutions and distinguishes between the roles of market infrastructures and of financial entities taking credit risks. With reference to the financial crisis, participants claim that standardized OTC-products are ideally integrated into centralized clearing; in terms of the settlement infrastructure, their preferred solution is an integration of both the cash and the securities leg within a single settlement platform.

The participants of the study seem to be well aware that the ideal post-trading system as described above is still a long way off. Nevertheless, they do have a clear view of what the industry could realistically look like in 2020: The experts characterize the **future European post-**

trading system as generally more integrated than today. Initiatives set off today will be finalized in 2020, such as the implementation of T2S that will speed up the European consolidation process. Giovannini barriers are expected to be partially removed: while the technical, market practice and legal barriers are effectively seen to be eliminated, the participants presume the removal of the fiscal barriers to require more time. Despite of increasing integration of the industry, the experts do not think that there will only remain one single settlement institution; nor do they agree that there will be one user-owned and user-governed settlement infrastructure. Post-trading is not believed to remain an area where excessive profits are achievable. In this environment, custodian banks that only serve domestic markets will be challenged. The main competitive battle field of agents, custodian banks, and CSDs will be custody services and corporate actions. CSDs are expected to create networks offering single access to clients and European clearing houses will provide services for complex products (like CDS).

The study participants propose a number of **measures to improve the post-trading system**:

- ☑ Ensure neutrality of clearing houses (no dependence on a single financial institution).
- ☑ Establish interoperability solutions between and among clearing houses and CSDs.
- ☑ Stronger cooperation between the post-trading industry and the issuers of innovative products to improve risk management.
- ☑ Financial infrastructures should focus on providing safe and secure services (concerning settlement/delivery, counterparty, and default).
- ☑ Financial infrastructures should ensure to cope with the rapid increase in volumes expected in times of a crisis.
- ☑ Elimination of legal Giovannini barriers.

- ☑ Maintain / foster competition and a level playing field for providers of securities services.
- ☑ Improve transparency of complex financial products (e.g. mortgages and CDS).
- ☑ Supervisory bodies should use a consistent set of standards and should communicate openly with each other.
- ☑ Improve regulation of rating agencies.
- ☑ Establish near-time transparency of OTC derivatives trades for regulators.
- ☑ Harmonization of the clearing houses' defaulting procedures and the underlying legal framework.

The experts emphasize the importance of **risk management** and **IT/IS** for the sound functioning of the post-trading system, both mutually interdependent with **regulation**. Therefore we asked the experts for the most important issues in these areas as these are part of the measures for improving the post-trading system or are important to achieve them.

Concerning **risk management** the experts state that the most important issues the post-trading system has to cope with are: The harmonization of legal certainty and of the rules of finality, default procedures, cancellation rules, and the implementation of highly secured processes as promoted by CPSS-IOSCO or by ESCB and CESR. The experts endorse the implementation of the Settlement Finality Directive and of the Financial Collateral Directive and call for a focus on transparency and on the stability of the legal and regulatory environment. Moreover, the optimization of collateral is mentioned. The experts also emphasize the need to introduce clearing houses for OTC-traded derivatives and to monitor the risk of derivatives issuers defaulting.

The area of **IT/IS** is still important for the post-trading system as the experts state that IT-systems continue to be an important competitive factor. Important IT/IS issues are the flexibility of the systems to meet the new regulatory and product-related requirements, the harmonization of protocols and communication standards, and the access to and interoperability of the systems. Moreover, IT-systems need to achieve real STP environments in order to reduce manual interventions. Real-time or event-triggered risk management and interaction between clearing houses are new important requirements for the clearing systems.

A few participants encouraged us to repeat this study on an annual basis. One expert pointed out that each asset class has its own rules and market structure which determine the future development of the post-trading system; an asset class specific view would therefore be beneficial when repeating this Delphi study.

5 References

Chlistalla, M. and Schaper, T. "Modifying the Balanced Scorecard for a Network Industry - The Case of the Clearing Industry", Software Services for e-Business and e-Society, Eds.: C. Godart, N. Gronau, S. Sharma and G. Canals; Nancy, 255-271, 2009.

Couper, M.R. "The Delphi Technique: characteristics and sequence model", Advances in Nursing Science, 7, 72-77, 1984.

Cox, P., Simpson, H., and Jones, L. "The Future of Clearing and Settlement in Europe", City Research Series, No 7, December 2005.

Dalkey, N.C. "The Delphi method: An experimental study of group opinion", Rand Corp., Santa Monica, CA, 1969.

European Central Bank "TARGET2-Securities". Frankfurt: European Central Bank. Available from: http://www.ecb.int/pub/pdf/other/ target2_securitiesen.pdf. Retrieved 22nd November 2009. December 2006.

European Central Bank "TARGET2-Securities – The T2S Blueprint", http://www.ecb.int/pub/pdf/other/t2sblueprint0703en.pdf. Retrieved November 22nd 2009. March 2007.

European Central Bank "Launch of the TARGET2-Securities project", Press Release 17.07.2008: http://www.ecb.int/press/pr/date/2008/html/pr080717.en.html. Retrieved August 27th 2008. July 2008.

European Central Bank "T2S Online. Quarterly Review 1/2009", 2009.

European Central Bank "OTC Derivatives and Post-Trading Infrastructures", 2009b.

Euroclear "Delivering a Domestic Market for Europe", July 2002.

European Commission "Directive 2004/39/EC of the European Parliament and of the Council of 21 April 2004 on markets in financial instruments amending Council Directives 85/611/EEC and 93/6/EEC and Directive 2000/12/EC of the European Parliament and of the Council and repealing Council Directive 93/22/EEC", 2004.

European Commission "Working document MARKT/SLG/G2(2005) D15283. Commission Services Working Document on Definitions of Post-Trading Activities", 2005.

European Commission "Draft working document on Post-Trading", 2006.

European Commission "COM(2009) 332 Ensuring efficient, safe and sound derivatives markets", 2009.

European Commission "SEC(2009) 905 Staff Working Paper", 2009b.

FESE, EACH, and ECSDA "The European Code of Conduct for Clearing and Settlement", 2006.

FESE "Share Ownership Structure in Europe", http://www.fese.be/_lib/files/Share Ownership_Survey_2007_Final.pdf. Retrieved November 4th 2009. December 2008.

Francotte, P. "Rising to the challenge of the crisis and change", The view from the CEO of Euroclear (14), 1-8, 2009.

Freeman, R.E. "Strategic Management: A Stakeholder Approach", Pitman, 1984.

Gibson J.M.E. "Using the Delphi to identify the content and context of nurses continuing professional development needs". Journal of Clinical Nursing 7, 451-459, 1998.

Giovannini Group "Cross-Border Clearing and Settlement Arrangements in the EU", 2001.

Giovannini Group "Second Report on EU Clearing and Settlement Arrangements", 2003.

Gomber, P. and Schaper, T. "Impact of Information Technology on Settlement Services for Equities", Market Study, 2007.

Goodman C.M. "The Delphi technique: a critique". Journal of Advanced Nursing 12, 729-734, 1987.

Hasson, F., Keeney, S., and McKeena, H. "Research Guidelines for the Delphi survey technique", Journal of Advanced Nursing, 32(4), 1008-1015, 2000.

Knieps, G. "Competition in the Post-Trade Markets: A Network Economic Analysis of the Securities Business", Journal of Industry, Competition and Trade, 6:1, 45–60, 2006.

Lannoo, K. and Valiante, D. "Integrating Europe's Back Office 10 years of turning in circles", ECMI Policy Brief, No. 13, June 2009.

LIBA, ESF, and ICMA "Letter to the ECB on Securities Sector Representation in T2S Committees", http://www.icma-group.org/market_practice/Advocacy/clearing_and_settlement/target2-securities.html. Retrieved April 27th 2007.

Link Up Markets "Link Up Markets", http://www.linkupmarkets.com/pdf/LinkUpMarkets_August2009.pdf. Retrieved October 20th 2009. August 2009.

McKenna, H.P. "The Delphi technique: a worthwhile approach for nursing? Journal of Advanced Nursing 19, 1221-1225, 1994.

Mitchell, R.K., Agle, B.R., and Wood, D.J. "Toward a Theory of Stakeholder Identification and Salience: Defining the Principle of Who and What really Counts", Academy of Management Review, 22(4), 853-886, 1997.

NERA "The direct costs of clearing and settlement: an EU-US comparison", Corporation of London City Research Series, No. 1, 2004.

NERA "The European Equities Post-Trading Industry: Assessing the Impact of Markets and Regulatory Changes", City Research Series, No 11, February 2007.

Oxera "Methodology for monitoring prices, costs, and volumes of trading and post-trading activities", Report prepared for the European Commission, July 2007.

Oxera "Monitoring prices, cost and volumes of trading and post-trading services", Report prepared for the European Commission, 2009.

Pirrong, C. "The Industrial Organization of Execution, Clearing and Settlement in Financial Markets", CFS, DBAG and EFL Research Conference, Frankfurt, 13th-14th June 2008.

Pirrong, C. "The Economics of Clearing in Derivatives Markets: Netting, Asymmetric Information, and the Sharing of Default Risks Through a Central Counterparty". University of Houston, Working Paper, 2009.

Schaper, T. "Trends in European Cross-Border Securities Settlement – TARGET2-Securities and the Code of Conduct", FinanceCom 2007 LNBIP 4, Ed: Veit, D.J., 50-65. Berlin: Springer, 2008.

Schaper, T. "Organizing Equity Exchanges", Proceedings of the 15th Americas Conference in Information Systems. San Francisco, USA, 2009.

Schaper, T. "Integrating Securities Settlement", Software Services for e-Business and e-Society, Eds.: C. Godart, N. Gronau, S. Sharma and G. Canals; Nancy, 385-399, 2009b.

Schaper, T. and Chlistalla, M. "Competitive Clearing in Europe - Development of a Performance Measurement System in a Changing Environment". The 6th NTU International Conference on Economics, Finance and Accounting; Taipei, Taiwan, 2008.

Schaper, T. and Chlistalla, M., "Deriving a Balanced Scorecard for the European Settlement Industry". Proceedings of the Fifteenth Americas Conference on Information Systems. San Francisco, California, 2009.

Schmiedel, H., Malkamäki, M., and Tarkka, J. "Economies of scale and technological development in securities depository and settlement systems", Journal of Banking & Finance, 30, 1783-1806, 2006.

Serifsoy, B. "Stock exchange business models and their operative performance", Journal of Banking & Finance 31, 2978-3012, 2007.

Serifsoy, B. and Weiß, M. "Settling for efficiency – A framework for the European securities transaction industry", Journal of Banking & Finance 31, 3034-3057, 2007.

Tumpel-Gugerell, G. "TARGET2-Securities: from vision to reality. The Eurosystem's contribution to an integrated securities market". EU Commission's Conference on: The EU's new regime for clearing and settlement in Europe. Brussels, 30th November 2006.

Wendt, F. "Intraday Margining of Central Counterparties: EU Practice and a Theoretical Evaluation of Benefits and Costs", Amsterdam: Netherlands Central Bank, 2006.

WFE "Report on Total Value of Share Trading". http://www.worldexchanges.org/ statistics/time-series/value-share-trading. Retrieved October 22nd 2009.

6 Glossary

CCBM2: Correspondent Central Banking Model 2, a new single platform for the management of Eurosystem collateral, which will be based on existing systems such as that of the Nationale Bank van België/Banque de Belgique and the De Nederlandsche Bank.

Clearing: The process of establishing settlement positions, possibly including the calculation of net positions, and the process of checking that securities, cash or both are available.

Central Counterparty Clearing: The process by which a third party interposes itself, directly or indirectly, between the transaction counterparties in order to assume their rights and obligations, acting as the direct or indirect buyer to every seller and the direct or indirect seller to every buyer.

Custodian: A specific custody services provider that provides custody services (and other additional services) as a third party to institutional clients. There are three kinds of custodians: local custodians, multi-market custodians, and global custodians.

Eurosystem: The Eurosystem, which comprises the European Central Bank and the national central banks of the Member States whose currency is the euro, is the monetary authority of the euro area.

TARGET2-Securities (T2S): A single platform for settling both cash and securities transactions in central bank money. T2S is solely a settlement service for all types of securities; custody and its associated services remain in the hands of central securities depositories.

(Book-entry) Settlement: The act of crediting and debiting the transferee's and transferor's accounts respectively, with the aim of completing a transaction in securities.

Multilateral Trading Facility (MTF): A multilateral system, operated by an investment firm or a market operator, which brings together multiple third-party buying and selling interests in financial instruments – in the system and in accordance with non-discretionary rules – in a way that results in a contract in accordance with the provisions of MiFID's authorization and operating conditions for investment firms.

7 List of Tables

Table 1: Literature Overview 15
Table 2: Questions and Hypotheses of the Delphi Study 38
Table 3: Participants and Response Rates 40
Table 4: General Hypotheses on the Efficiency of the Post-Trading
System 43
Table 5: Reasons for the Efficiency of the domestic Post-Trading
System in Europe 44
Table 6: Reasons for the Inefficiency of the domestic Post-Trading
System in Europe 46
Table 7: Reasons for the Efficiency of the cross-Border Post-Trading
System in Europe 47
Table 8: Reasons for the Inefficiency of the cross-Border Post-
Trading System in Europe: Giovannini Barriers 48
Table 9: Reasons for the Inefficiency of the cross-Border Post-
Trading System in Europe: Organization and Competition 49
Table 10: Reasons for the Inefficiency of the cross-Border Post-
Trading System in Europe: Processes and IT 50
Table 11: Reasons for the Inefficiency of the cross-Border Post-
Trading System in Europe: Risk Management 50
Table 12: Reasons for the Inefficiency of the cross-Border Post-
Trading System in Europe: Regulation 52
Table 13: Reasons for the Inefficiency of the cross-Border Post-
Trading System in Europe: Other 52
Table 14: Characterization of the ideal European Post-Trading
System: Giovannini Barriers 54
Table 15: Characterization of the ideal European Post-Trading
System: Market Organization 57
Table 16: Characterization of the ideal European Post-Trading
System: Processes and Market Infrastructure 60

Table 17: Characterization of the ideal European Post-Trading System: Regulation 62
Table 18: The European Post-Trading System in 2020 63
Table 19: The European Post-Trading System in 2020: Market Organization 66
Table 20: The European Post-Trading System in 2020: Governance and Business Development 68
Table 21: The European Post-Trading System in 2020: TARGET2-Securities..72
Table 22: The European Post-Trading System in 2020: Giovannini Barriers..72
Table 23: The European Post-Trading System in 2020: Integration 73
Table 24: Measures to improve the Post-Trading System in Context of the financial Crisis 75
Table 25: Measures to improve the Post-Trading System in Context of the financial Crisis: Organization...76
Table 26: Measures to improve the Post-Trading System in Context of the financial Crisis: Infrastructures 77
Table 27: Measures to improve the Post-Trading System in Context of the financial Crisis: Risk 78
Table 28: Measures to improve the Post-Trading System in Context of the financial Crisis: IT 79
Table 29: Measures to improve the Post-Trading System in Context of the financial Crisis: Regulation 81
Table 30: Most important Risk Management Issues the Post-Trading System needs to cope with 84
Table 31: Most important Risk Management Issues the Post-Trading System needs to cope with: General Statements 84
Table 36: Most important IT/IS Issues the Post-Trading System needs to cope with: General Statements 90
Table 38: Most important IT/IS Issues the Post-Trading System needs to cope with: IT-system Provisioning....................................92

Table 39: Most important IT/IS Issues the Post-Trading System
   needs to cope with: Communication 93
Table 40: Most important IT/IS Issues the Post-Trading System
   needs to cope with: Other 94

8 List of Figures

Figure 1: Flow-related and Stock-related Activities in the Securities Trading Value Chain (adapted from European Central Bank 2007) 18
Figure 2: Instruction Flows for a domestic Equity Transaction (Giovannini Group 2001) 19
Figure 3: Instruction Flows for a cross-Border Equity Transaction (Giovannini Group 2001) 21
Figure 4: Selected Equity Market Infrastructures in Europe (adapted from Cox, Simpson, and Jones 2005) 24
Figure 5: Integration of Payment and Settlement System with TARGET2 and TARGET2-Securities (European Central Bank 2006, Tumpel-Gugerell 2006) 27
Figure 6: Link Up Markets Interaction Channels (Link Up Markets 2009) 28
Figure 7: The Single Settlement Engine (Euroclear 2002) 30
Figure 8: Stakeholders of the European Post-Trading System 35
Figure 9: Screenshot of the Online-Survey 36
Figure 10: 5-Item Likert Scale 41
Figure 11: Distribution of Answers regarding Hypothesis 1-09 45
Figure 12: Distribution of Answers regarding Hypothesis 1-08 46
Figure 13: Distribution of Answers regarding Hypothesis 1-29 51
Figure 14: Distribution of Answers regarding Hypothesis 2-03 55
Figure 15: Distribution of Answers regarding Hypothesis 2-06 56
Figure 16: Distribution of Answers regarding Hypothesis 2-16 58
Figure 17: Distribution of Answers regarding Hypothesis 2-20 58
Figure 18: Distribution of Answers regarding Hypothesis 2-27 61
Figure 19: Distribution of Answers regarding Hypothesis 3-08 64
Figure 20: Distribution of Answers regarding Hypothesis 3-12 65
Figure 21: Distribution of Answers regarding Hypothesis 3-28 69

Figure 22: Distribution of Answers regarding Hypothesis 3-29 70
Figure 23: Distribution of Answers regarding Hypothesis 3-27 70
Figure 24: Distribution of Answers regarding Hypothesis 5-01 83
Figure 25: Milestones and Projects in the Post-Trading Industry 96
Figure 26: The Way towards a future European Post-Trading System 98

9 List of Abbreviations

CCBM2	Collateral Central Bank Management
CCP	Central Counterparty
CDS	Credit Default Swap
CESAME	Clearing and Settlement Advisory and Monitoring Experts Group
CESR	Committee of European Securities Regulators
CPSS	Committee on Payment and Settlement Systems
CSD	Central Securities Depository
DVP/RVP	Delivery versus Payment / Receive versus Payment
ECB	European Central Bank
EMCF	European Multilateral Clearing Facility
ESCB	European System of Central Banks
ESES	Euroclear Settlement for Euronext-zone Securities
FIX	Financial Information eXchange
FSAP	Financial Services Action Plan
ICSD	International Central Securities Depository
IOSCO	International Organization of Securities Commissions
ISO	International Organization for Standardization
MiFID	Markets in Financial Instruments Directive
MTF	Multilateral Trading Facility
OTC	Over The Counter
R2	Round 2

R3	Round 3
SSE	Single Settlement Engine
STD	Standard Deviation
STP	Straight Through Processing
SWIFT	Society for Worldwide Interbank Financial Telecommunication
TARGET	Trans-European Automated Real-time Gross settlement Express Transfer System
T2S	TARGET2-Securities

10 Complete Results of Round Two and Round Three

Question 1:

	General hypotheses on efficiency of the post-trading system:	Mean R2	STD R2	n R2 (N=36)	Mean R3	STD R3	n R3 (N=40)
1-01	Post-trading at the national level is efficient.	1.91	0.95	35	1.95	0.96	40
1-02	Post-trading at the intra-system level is efficient.	2.44	1.13	32	2.45	1.13	38
1-03	Cross-border post-trading is efficient.	4.00	1.03	35	4.05	1.00	39
1-04	European post-trading in general is efficient.	3.28	0.97	36	3.25	0.93	40
	Domestic post-trading is efficient due to						
1-05	High settlement rates (Low amount of value of failed transactions).	1.91	0.83	34	1.95	0.87	38
1-06	Technical reliability (e.g. in case of the Lehman Brothers default).	1.74	0.75	34	1.79	0.78	38
1-07	Financial infrastructures have provided tools for effective risk mitigation (e.g. employing strict DVP/RVP).	1.97	0.83	34	1.87	0.62	38

	Domestic post-trading is inefficient due to:							
1-08	Vertical integration of trading, clearing, and settlement.	3.48	1.50	33	3.50	1.34	39	
1-09	No horizontal competition in trading, clearing, and settlement.	2.97	1.47	32	3.03	1.27	39	
	Cross-border post-trading is efficient due to:							
1-10	High settlement rates (Low amount of value of failed transactions).	2.90	0.99	30	3.03	0.92	35	
1-11	Technical reliability (e.g. in case of the Lehman Brothers default).	2.80	1.00	30	2.80	0.87	35	
	Cross-border post-trading is inefficient due to:							
1-12	Financial infrastructures have provided tools for effective risk mitigation (e.g. employing strict DVP/RVP).	3.03	0.93	30	2.97	0.89	35	
1-13	Remaining technical (Giovannini) barriers (too many proprietary systems, standards, and technical solutions).	1.94	0.84	35	1.85	0.74	39	
1-14	Remaining market practice (Giovannini) barriers.	1.97	0.75	35	1.90	0.68	39	

1-15	Remaining legal (Giovannini) barriers.	1.51	0.74	35	1.51	0.76	39
1-16	Remaining fiscal (Giovannini) barriers.	1.74	0.89	35	1.71	0.84	39
1-17	Too many levels of infrastructure which offer redundant services.	2.64	1.08	33	2.59	1.09	37
1-18	Long chains of financial intermediaries and infrastructures.	2.23	1.05	35	2.08	0.96	39
1-19	The current infrastructure is too fragmented.	2.20	1.05	35	2.13	1.00	39
1-20	Lack of interoperability between financial infrastructures.	2.17	1.22	35	2.13	1.06	39
1-21	Limited competition.	2.26	1.20	35	2.28	1.17	39
1-22	Some financial intermediaries and infrastructures generate revenues from the inefficiencies.	1.70	0.85	33	1.70	0.85	37
1-23	Too much manual intervention in some post-trading processes.	2.50	0.88	32	2.56	0.88	36
1-24	Back office costs arise for financial institutions for connecting to each of the different post-trading systems.	1.85	0.78	34	1.84	0.72	38

1-25	New clearing houses are not always offering an equivalent level of risk coverage and market-protection as the incumbent clearing houses.	2.85	1.08	34	2.79	1.07	38
1-26	Fee decreases started by some players lead the post-trading industry towards higher risk.	3.32	0.98	34	3.42	0.92	38
1-27	Lack of standardization in risk management.	2.59	0.82	34	2.65	0.86	37
1-28	MiFID increased the complexity of trading and post-trading.	2.74	1.16	34	2.71	1.09	38
1-29	Not enough focus of the European policy makers on efficiency.	2.85	1.30	33	2.89	1.31	37
1-30	Not enough focus of the European policy makers on safety.	3.09	1.08	34	3.13	1.04	38
1-31	Pan-European regulation allows regulatory arbitrage.	2.44	0.84	32	2.54	0.90	37
1-32	European regulation is influenced by political agendas which lead to compromise-based solutions that reflect the political reality rather than the most efficient solutions.	2.03	0.98	33	1.92	0.86	37
1-33	Financial intermediaries have more power than issuers and investors.	2.41	1.13	37	2.45	1.13	38

| 1-34 | Long chains of intermediaries make the passing of information between the issuer and the investor inefficient. | 2.51 | 1.09 | 38 | 2.44 | 1.10 | 39 |
| 1-35 | Settlement failures and the way they are treated (allowing delivery failures to go on almost endlessly). | 2.90 | 1.01 | 30 | 2.74 | 1.07 | 35 |

Question 2:

	The ideal European post-trading system would be characterized by:	Mean R2	STD R2	n R2 (N=36)	Mean R3	STD R3	n R3 (N=40)
2-01	A system based on competition and market innovation on each layer of the value chain as existent today.	2.21	0.84	38	2.21	0.84	38
2-02	Decentralized financial infrastructures to avoid (systemic) risk accumulation.	2.74	0.98	38	2.74	0.98	38
2-03	Vertical disintegration of trading, clearing, and settlement.	2.68	1.25	37	2.68	1.25	37
2-04	Access and interoperability in the area of trading, clearing, and settlement.	1.65	0.72	37	1.65	0.72	37
2-05	Freedom of choice for investors with regard to trading, clearing, settlement, and custody.	1.65	0.86	37	1.65	0.86	37
2-06	One 'domestic' European post-trading infrastructure.	3.16	1.28	37	3.16	1.28	37
2-07	Elimination of legal (Giovannini) barriers.	1.56	0.72	39	1.56	0.72	39
2-08	Elimination of technical and market practice (Giovannini) barriers.	1.64	0.71	39	1.64	0.71	39
2-09	Elimination of fiscal (Giovannini) barriers.	1.55	0.72	39	1.55	0.72	39
2-10	Competition on the trading level to keep prices low and innovation high.	1.79	0.84	38	1.79	0.84	38

2-11	Clearing houses separated from exchanges.	2.53	1.14	33	2.38	1.04	37
2-12	Two to three clearing houses, all of which interoperable to guarantee choice of clearing venue.	2.45	1.03	34	2.29	0.96	38
2-13	Competition on the clearing level to keep prices low and innovation high.	1.97	0.77	34	1.92	0.75	38
2-14	Large clearing houses (to provide efficient netting and collateral management).	2.35	0.91	32	2.36	0.93	36
2-15	Settlement co-location in one single settlement location.	2.36	1.11	27	2.57	1.19	30
2-16	One European security register (including end customers and nominees).	2.25	1.19	33	2.51	1.37	37
2-17	Usage of central bank money for every settlement.	2.45	1.12	34	2.50	1.13	38
2-18	Integration of both the cash and the securities leg in a single settlement platform.	2.03	1.00	32	2.00	0.97	35
2-19	Exactly one clearing house and one CSD.	3.88	1.21	33	4.03	1.12	37
2-20	Clearing houses and CSDs that operate on a not-for-profit basis or under constrained profit rules.	3.42	1.43	32	3.33	1.35	36
2-21	T2S that is not operated by the Eurosystem.	3.30	1.15	31	3.18	1.09	34
2-22	A mandatory participation in T2S.	3.34	1.17	30	3.42	1.15	33
2-23	Competition in asset servicing between CSDs and custodian banks to keep prices low and innovation high.	2.47	1.38	35	2.41	1.16	39

2-24	The ability for investors to hold assets directly in a central system.	2.50	0.99	35	2.46	1.00	39
2-25	A regulatory framework that focuses on functions rather than on institutions.	1.94	0.90	34	1.95	0.90	38
2-26	A regulatory framework that distinguishes between the roles of market infrastructures and of financial entities taking credit risks.	2.00	0.75	34	2.00	0.84	38
2-27	A regulatory framework that includes custodian banks in the requirements applying to clearing houses and CSDs.	2.39	1.09	34	2.50	1.20	38
2-28	Rules to regulate 'cherry picking' in trading and post-trading.	2.29	0.82	32	2.28	0.81	36
2-29	Direct access from issuer to investor.	2.76	1.12	30	2.65	1.10	34
2-30	Standardized OTC-products integrated into centralized clearing.	2.06	0.86	34	1.97	0.85	38

Question 3:

	In 2020...	Mean R2	STD R2	n R2 (N=36)	Mean R3	STD R3	n R3 (N=40)
3-01	European post-trading will be more integrated than today.	1.66	0.65	33	1.54	0.51	37
3-02	There will be no single market achieved as the current global financial crisis prevents the necessary investments.	3.38	1.21	33	3.43	1.09	37
3-03	The number of exchanges will be smaller.	2.58	1.20	34	2.42	1.13	38
3-04	The number of Multilateral Trading Facilities will be smaller than today.	2.50	1.16	33	2.32	1.11	37
3-05	The European post-trading system will consist of two to three clearing houses.	2.55	0.99	32	2.50	0.94	36
3-06	Consolidation of clearing houses will take place through aggressive competition.	2.48	0.91	34	2.45	0.83	38
3-07	The European post-trading system will consist of less CSDs than today.	2.06	0.95	33	2.03	0.90	37
3-08	The European post-trading system will consist of one single settlement institution.	3.03	1.35	33	3.24	1.30	37
3-09	The number of custodian banks will be smaller.	2.44	0.91	33	2.24	0.86	37

3-10	The European post-trading system will consist of a high number of access providers to clearing and settlement institutions.	2.87	0.88	32	2.81	0.86	36
3-11	There will be one user-owned and user-governed settlement infrastructure.	3.48	1.15	34	3.61	1.10	38
3-12	The entire European post-trading system will come under the governance from regulators or central banks.	3.55	1.18	33	3.49	1.22	37
3-13	The pace at which consolidation will take place will be determined not only by market forces, but also by political interventions.	2.25	0.98	33	2.14	0.89	37
3-14	The owners of post-trading infrastructures will be vertically integrated trading platforms.	3.39	0.72	32	3.47	0.81	36
3-15	The owners of post-trading infrastructures will be financial intermediaries.	2.84	0.72	35	2.78	0.76	36
3-16	Post-trading will continue to be an area where excessive profits are achievable.	3.58	1.06	34	3.66	1.10	38
3-17	Global custody will be the most profitable post-trading segment.	2.66	0.83	33	2.57	0.83	37
3-18	The main competitive battle field of agents, custodian banks and, CSDs will be custody services and corporate actions.	1.91	0.93	33	2.00	0.94	37

3-19	Clearing and settlement infrastructures will improve their services through cooperation rather than through competition.	2.64	0.93	33	2.68	0.93	38
3-20	Custodian banks that only serve domestic markets will be particularly challenged.	1.91	0.96	34	1.89	0.92	38
3-21	Settlement services will have become a standardized commodity with little room for customization and innovation.	3.35	0.91	32	3.17	1.00	36
3-48	Custody services will have become a standardized commodity with little room for customization and innovation.	3.35	0.91	31	3.49	0.89	35
3-22	CSDs will start providing more value added services.	2.00	0.84	33	2.03	0.87	37
3-23	Complex institutional transactions will be niches for specialized post-trade providers.	2.09	0.86	33	2.19	0.91	37
3-24	T2S will be live.	1.72	0.81	33	1.75	0.77	36
3-25	T2S will start off as a provider of settlement-only functions but will add on other functions as it develops.	2.72	1.20	33	2.58	1.16	36
3-26	The launch of T2S will speed up the European consolidation process.	2.03	1.23	33	1.89	1.01	36
3-27	T2S will have blurred the differences between CSDs and custodian banks.	2.81	1.28	33	2.83	1.21	36
3-28	T2S will have reduced the costs of cross-border trade settlement.	2.22	1.26	33	2.25	1.20	36

3-29	T2S will maintain the efficiency of domestic trade settlement.	2.55	1.31	32	2.63	1.29	35
3-30	T2S will have led to a legal and fiscal harmonization in Europe.	2.56	1.16	32	2.63	1.14	35
3-31	The overall cost of clearing and settlement will not reduce after T2S because CSDs will still provide custody and corporate action processing (and will retain settlement information in their systems).	3.19	1.05	33	3.11	1.06	36
3-32	CSDs will use the same underlying IT infrastructures: T2S for settlement and private infrastructures for the other services.	2.42	0.62	32	2.37	0.65	35
3-33	T2S will contribute to a borderless and seamless European post-trading system.	2.25	1.19	33	2.22	1.05	36
3-34	Collateral Central Bank Management (CCBM2) will contribute to a borderless and seamless European post-trading system.	2.25	0.80	32	2.26	0.78	35
3-35	The technical (Giovannini) barriers will be eliminated.	2.18	1.04	34	2.16	0.97	38
3-36	The market practice (Giovannini) barriers will be eliminated.	2.33	1.05	34	2.26	0.95	38
3-37	The legal (Giovannini) barriers will be eliminated.	2.88	1.08	34	2.92	1.05	38
3-38	The fiscal (Giovannini) barriers will be eliminated.	3.52	0.91	34	3.53	0.89	38

3-39	Price transparency of clearing and settlement will be implemented.	2.16	1.08	33	2.11	1.02	37
3-40	Access and interoperability of clearing and settlement will be implemented.	2.13	0.94	33	2.14	0.95	37
3-41	Service unbundling and account separation of clearing and settlement will be implemented.	2.25	1.02	33	2.22	1.03	37
3-42	There will be an EU-wide regulation of post-trading.	2.47	1.11	33	2.38	0.98	37
3-43	European clearing houses will be supervised by a central European supervisory authority rather than by national authorities.	2.59	1.19	33	2.57	1.14	37
3-44	European clearing houses will provide services for complex financial products (like CDS).	2.00	0.92	33	1.95	0.81	37
3-45	CSDs will create networks offering single access to clients.	1.88	0.71	33	1.89	0.70	37
3-46	The integration between European and US post-trading infrastructures will be established.	3.18	1.01	34	3.16	1.05	38
3-47	The integration between European and Asian post-trading infrastructures will be established.	3.48	1.03	34	3.45	1.03	38

Question 4:

	Measures to improve the post-trading system in context of the financial crisis are:	Mean R2	STD R2	n R2 (N=36)	Mean R3	STD R3	n R3 (N=40)
4-01	There is no need for action: Financial infrastructures have been very robust in the financial crisis.	3.18	1.09	35	3.18	1.17	39
4-02	Focus on the soundness of the post-trading system.	2.26	0.93	34	2.24	0.97	38
4-03	Reduce the system's dependence on banks in view of the fragility they have demonstrated (some financial conglomerates are too big to fail).	2.32	0.91	35	2.33	0.93	39
4-04	Consolidation of financial infrastructures.	2.56	0.96	35	2.64	1.01	39
4-05	Maintain the separation of different roles of financial infrastructures and intermediaries.	2.30	0.88	34	2.18	0.73	38
4-06	Consideration of risk aspects in the management compensations of the post-trading industry.	2.24	1.26	33	2.38	1.09	37

4-07	Ensure neutrality of clearing houses (no dependence on a single financial institution).	2.00	1.00	34	1.95	0.87	38
4-08	Establish interoperability solutions between and among clearing houses and CSDs.	1.71	0.72	34	1.89	0.86	38
4-09	Introduction of a central post-trading infrastructure to maximize economies of scale.	2.94	1.28	33	3.16	1.07	37
4-10	Introduction of T2S to improve liquidity and collateral management in the euro-zone.	2.21	1.17	32	2.51	1.17	35
4-11	Introduction of CCBM2 to improve liquidity and collateral management in the euro-zone.	1.91	1.03	31	2.12	0.88	34
4-12	Improve the traceability of securities (e.g. outstanding deliveries and settled instructions).	2.03	0.90	34	2.11	1.01	38
4-13	Integration of OTC derivatives into a centralized clearing house.	2.21	1.01	34	2.21	0.99	38
4-14	Ensure diversification of clearing houses in terms of customer groups and products.	2.59	1.02	34	2.74	0.95	38

4-15	Stronger cooperation between the post-trading industry and the issuers of innovative products to improve risk management.	1.88	0.89	33	1.92	0.80	37
4-16	Financial infrastructures should focus on providing safe and secure services (concerning settlement/delivery, counterparty, and default).	1.67	0.78	34	1.63	0.75	38
4-17	Reduction of post-trade processing time.	2.09	1.03	34	2.24	1.00	38
4-18	Increased use of central bank money.	1.97	0.80	34	2.11	0.73	38
4-19	Harmonization of collateral and margining rules.	1.94	0.89	34	2.16	1.03	38
4-20	Financial infrastructures should increase operational risk management.	2.03	0.80	35	2.08	0.84	39
4-21	Financial infrastructures should ensure to cope with the rapid increase in volumes expected in times of a crisis.	1.71	0.84	34	1.92	0.88	38
4-22	Financial infrastructures should operate in a near real-time mode so that users always have a near real-time view of their positions.	1.91	0.93	34	2.03	1.00	38

4-23	Elimination of legal (Giovannini) barriers.	1.74	0.79	34	1.84	0.89	38
4-24	Avoid competition between clearing houses in terms of risk management by voluntary industry agreement.	2.62	1.16	33	2.73	0.96	37
4-25	Avoid competition between clearing houses in terms of risk management by regulation / supervision.	2.38	1.28	33	2.54	1.10	37
4-26	Maintain / foster competition and a level playing field for providers of securities services.	1.76	0.61	34	1.74	0.55	38
4-27	A directive can be a driver for an efficient single European market.	2.44	1.16	34	2.63	1.13	38
4-28	Extended MiFID to post-trading services.	3.29	1.34	34	3.43	1.17	37
4-29	Intervention of authorities to improve efficiency if the markets do not make enough progress (e.g. in context of the European Code of Conduct for Clearing and Settlement).	2.41	1.18	34	2.50	1.03	38
4-30	Near-time transparency of OTC derivatives trades for regulators.	1.88	0.82	32	1.92	0.73	38

4-31	Improve transparency of complex financial products (e.g. mortgages and CDS).	1.65	0.77	34	1.68	0.70	38
4-32	Supervisory bodies should use a consistent set of standards and should communicate openly with each other.	1.64	0.65	34	1.66	0.67	38
4-33	Review systemically relevant functions (e.g. through market share or functionality such as high volume internalization) with a view to applying consistent regulation.	1.97	0.88	33	2.03	0.76	37
4-34	Harmonization of the clearing houses' defaulting procedures and the underlying legal framework.	1.85	0.99	34	1.92	0.97	38
4-35	Improve regulation of rating agencies.	1.41	0.70	33	1.43	0.60	37

Question 5:

	The most important risk management issues the post-trading system needs to cope with are:	Mean R2	STD R2	n R2 (N=36)	Mean R3	STD R3	n R3 (N=40)
5-01	There is no need for action: The current financial infrastructure is very stable.	3.47	1.02	33	3.57	1.07	37
5-02	Fee reductions not based on efficiency improvements are a danger.	2.73	1.13	33	2.70	1.02	37
5-03	There is a risk that competition and innovation are at the expense of safety.	2.45	1.15	34	2.45	1.11	38
5-04	Transparency (financial institutions and infrastructures need to be able to identify their customer, their counterparty, and the instrument they have invested in).	1.70	0.81	34	1.61	0.72	38
5-05	Change management of the large number of infrastructure reform projects.	2.43	0.74	34	2.44	0.70	34
5-06	Separation of notary function and financial services provided by CSDs (notary function should not be put at risk).	2.48	1.09	32	2.54	1.07	35
5-07	Implementation of highly secured processes as promoted by CPSS-IOSCO or by ESCB and CESR.	2.00	0.91	32	2.00	0.85	34
5-08	Elimination of settlement risks by increasing the usage of central bank money.	2.15	0.80	33	2.22	0.82	37

5-09	Optimizing financial institutions' collateral management.	1.97	0.78	32	1.92	0.65	36
5-10	Riskier derivatives need to be settled on a trade-by-trade basis, not in a netting system.	3.10	1.21	29	3.12	1.19	33
5-11	Risk evaluation of illiquid securities (due to the divergence between fundamental value and market value).	2.09	0.77	33	2.11	0.77	37
5-12	Financial institutions and intermediaries need timely clearing and settlement including related reports to determine risks and account positions precisely.	1.73	0.57	34	1.71	0.52	38
5-13	CSDs are exposed to operational risk events and should therefore ensure state-of-the-art operational resilience.	1.82	0.77	34	1.61	0.64	38
5-14	Harmonization of legal certainty.	1.58	0.66	34	1.47	0.60	38
5-15	Harmonization of rules of finality, default procedures, and cancellation rules.	1.53	0.57	33	1.43	0.50	37
5-16	Implementation of the Settlement Finality Directive and Financial Collateral Directive.	1.57	0.68	31	1.59	0.86	34
5-17	Stability of the legal and regulatory environment.	1.54	0.65	34	1.55	0.60	38

5-18	Prevent financial infrastructures from taking too much credit risk (when competing with financial institutions) by regulation.	2.19	1.00	32	2.22	0.93	36
5-19	Establish a fast reacting international task force in case of failure of systemically relevant market infrastructures.	2.10	1.08	32	2.14	1.02	36
5-20	Regulate OTC markets by similar rules as regulated markets.	2.69	1.15	33	2.62	1.16	37
5-21	Enhancement of linked settlement of OTC-traded equities.	2.32	0.87	32	2.31	0.82	36
5-22	Introduction of clearing houses for OTC-traded derivatives.	1.75	0.57	33	1.78	0.58	37
5-23	Monitor the risk of derivatives issuers defaulting.	1.81	0.69	33	1.84	0.76	37

Question 6:

	The most important IT/ IS issues the post-trading system needs to cope with are:	Mean R2	STD R2	n R2 (N=36)	Mean R3	STD R3	n R3 (N=40)
6-01	IT-systems are not a competitive factor in the post-trading landscape anymore.	3.66	1.07	33	3.78	0.89	37
6-02	Risk due to the concentration in the post-trading industry.	2.90	0.84	33	2.95	0.78	37
6-03	To establish links from legacy systems to T2S and CCBM2.	2.13	0.90	31	2.12	0.98	34
6-04	Increasing IT investments due to dynamics on post-trading markets.	2.16	0.85	33	2.11	0.84	37
6-05	Scarcity of resources (staff and IT) when IT-systems need to be upgraded in all parts of the post-trading area at the same time (e.g. due to T2S).	2.03	0.94	30	2.03	0.87	34
6-06	Consolidation of IT platforms.	2.24	0.95	30	2.12	0.77	34
6-07	Availability.	2.63	1.03	31	2.51	0.98	35

6-08	Flexibility / modularity of systems to meet new regulatory and product-related requirements.	1.94	0.68	32	1.83	0.51	36
6-09	Scalability (capacity to deal with peak volumes).	2.23	0.84	32	2.08	0.77	36
6-10	Outsourcing of IT infrastructure (or services) outside the EU.	2.55	1.03	31	2.63	1.00	35
6-11	Outsourcing of IT infrastructure (or services) outside the EU.	2.90	0.98	31	3.09	0.95	35
6-12	IT-systems need to achieve a real STP environment in order to reduce manual intervention.	1.74	0.68	32	1.72	0.61	36
6-13	Access and Interoperability (analog to the Code of Conduct).	1.87	0.81	32	1.89	0.82	36
6-14	Harmonization of protocols and communication standards.	1.55	0.57	32	1.69	0.82	36
6-15	Establishment and implementation of FIX as standard for messaging.	3.07	1.11	28	3.09	1.15	32
6-16	Establishment and implementation of SWIFT / ISO as standard for messaging.	2.30	0.99	31	2.26	0.85	35

6-17	Availability of old message formats for user convenience.	3.30	1.12	31	3.37	0.97	35
6-18	Establishment of secure internet connectivity for messaging.	2.26	0.89	32	2.39	1.02	36
6-19	Real-time or event-triggered risk management.	1.81	0.74	33	1.84	0.76	37
6-20	Interaction between clearing houses and customers (for margin payments or collateral provision) and between linked clearing houses.	1.97	0.71	32	1.89	0.67	36

ibidem-Verlag

Melchiorstr. 15

D-70439 Stuttgart

info@ibidem-verlag.de

www.ibidem-verlag.de
www.ibidem.eu
www.edition-noema.de
www.autorenbetreuung.de